CW00672719

Garden of the Jaguar

Garden of the Jaguar

*Travel, plants and people
in Chiapas, Mexico*

Bernardine Coverley

Copyright © 2009 by Bernardine Coverley

First published 2009
by Green Bee Books
website: www.bernardinecoverley.co.uk
email: bernardine5@btinternet.com

Book design by Bridget Morley

Printed in Great Britain by the MPG Books Group,
Bodmin and King's Lynn

A catalogue record for this book is available
from the British Library

ISBN 978-0-9564271-0-6

ACKNOWLEDGEMENTS

Foremost, I want to acknowledge Trudy and Frans Blom, Na Bolom's founders, courageous pioneers who loved the forests but knew people and the landscape were linked to each other. They put their beliefs into action, imperfect human beings, as we all are, and braver for that. A big thank you to Na Bolom for my time there. In my days in the garden, Manuel, Javier, Humberto, were my valued guides and guardians. Warm hearted Elisa M. Caire remains my friend and inspiration.

Of the many other friends and colleagues in Chiapas who I came to know and value, and with whom I had enjoyable and illuminating times, the following are important: Beatriz Mijangos Zenteno, F. Sanchez Balderas, I.H. Roome, Cecilia Hernandez Morales, Cisco Dietz, Kevin P. Groark, Robert and Mimi Laughlin, Juan Castillo, Christine Pauwels, Carolina Hoch, Megan O'Neil, Marlou and Bolly, Fredy Lopez Arevalo, Maruch and Rosita.

In the forest, I learnt from Atanasio, Enrique Paniagua and his family, particularly Margarita and Kuti. In town, Jorge and Romeo raised my level of Spanish with laughter and deep conversation.

Many of those I met or worked with appear as themselves, others I have renamed or fused into one simply for narrative understanding. I trust they will understand the affection with which I have recorded them.

At home in my wooded valley in Suffolk, thanks are gratefully offered to all those who encouraged me to bring this book into being, Jackie Reiter, Mary Jane Riley, Sarah Bower, Mary Allen, Chris van Melzen, Tessa West. Bridget Morley's patience in final design moments was invaluable. Thank you also to Patrick Marnham whose experience of Latin America and advice was a generous contribution.

This book is for anyone who has a passion for plants or even the tiniest bit of wilderness, ever walked in a wood or nurtured a window box. I have followed the Bloms' example and put my effort here in the hope of inspiring others to observe the natural world around us.

Through making this book I have come to know the World Land Trust and its work to preserve tropical forests for the plant and wildlife and thus for us all.

For my family

fer snake hiliana los raices
O'pok -spines
macho
mujer
no tiene
pinas

was write had: had stomega

piece of wood chips
jugo De huga
cut + use juice
Sak suku chu - for war
sores + cuts.

Contents

Introduction

My 60th birthday lunch was a family gathering outside among the flowers. Sitting at a long table in my garden, food laid out on a white cloth decorated with jugs of fat pink roses and marguerite daisies, I celebrated in the best company; children, grandchildren, closest friends. Just enough people so we could all see and talk to each other.

'So what now?' someone asked.

'Mmm...' I said, 'I've always wanted to go back to Mexico.'

I thought about the decade that had just come to end, and ahead, the beginning of the later part of my life, the sixties, my sixties. I hesitated before writing later, rather than late, or even last. But the question in my mind was, 'What do I want for the rest of my life?' If I didn't find out now, I would no longer be capable. As a veteran of Greenham Common demonstrations and a mass trespass on the Newbury bypass, I reminded myself of the old demo marching mantra of, 'What do we want and when do we want it? Now, Now, Now!'

What did I want? Before I could tell myself it was too late answers came: to speak another language well and to be a good gardener. I spoke adequate French and Spanish and gardened already but in a hurried, if often productive way. Vegetables were my speciality, and if I threw in some marigold seeds or sweet peas, I might be lucky. I wanted to build on good enough and find a deeper, richer knowledge.

My life lacked time to develop skills, to learn to do well what I had done over so many years out of enthusiasm and conviction. I grew organic vegetables for my family in the 70s, and my favourite photograph is a black and white print of a trug displaying the beauty of my produce; potatoes, beetroot, lettuce, parsley, all burstingly fresh. This is the picture I would have as a framed memorial, not a portrait as such, like those on Latin American graves, but a true representation of me even so.

As the children grew up I continued to cultivate any patch of earth whether it was a vegetable plot and fruit cage in Sussex on the edge of Ashdown Forest or window boxes and potted geraniums in London. Once I carried a young plum tree on the bus from Wood Green in North London to a back yard in Archway. After the children left home I moved back to the country, to a rural area of East Anglia and a large old fashioned garden with flowers, vegetables and fruit trees.

Gardening was a compulsion, but I needed to find a way that made me feel I was cooperating with the natural world, not squeezing it in round the rest of my life, trying to catch up with seasons and growth spurts, keeping grass under control and hedges cut and orderly.

I wanted to reclaim the childhood feeling when I played among the wild flowers and grasses of post war bomb sites. The magical places that we called 'the dumps' were full of plants that touched the senses. Pink rosebay willow grew among the rubble, scratchy goosegrass heads crept up your sleeve or your back when someone slipped one between your dress and your cardigan, cleavers miraculously clung to you. And all the beetles and spiders that lived among them carried on busily at eye level if I squatted down chewing a sweet grass stem.

My mother's garden looked out over the dumps from a flat roof we reached by steps up and through the big bathroom window. Tins of earth, old basins and barrels were the foundation of her garden and from these bloomed snapdragons and lobelia in the sort of cluttered profusion of colour that predated any design theories. A garden that seems in retrospect to represent that happy naturalness of childhood, and my mother's spontaneity and need, a young Irish woman from a farm living in the bombstricken inner city.

Even sent away to a second-rate boarding school in the country, the weekly crocodile walk to The Nower consoled me for the imprisonment of the convent. The Nower was a slope of old meadow topped by bracken and a wood of oaks and beech, with thickets of hazel and bramble. Once through the gate, the little girls in brown uniforms broke free and spent a few hours playing rough, rolling in the bracken, hunting for beech nuts and blackberries and vinegary sorrel. Best of all were quiet moments prone in the grass looking close up at harebells, lady's slipper, the brown seeds of quaking grass. The Nower provided green medicine. Soul solace.

My next birthday was in San Cristobal de Las Casas, Mexico, in the southern state of Chiapas. I was working in the gardens of Na Bolom, a Mexican charity, founded in the 1950s, and dedicated to the conservation of one of the most biodiverse places in the world, the Lacandon rainforest. My guests, and friends, at this birthday ate pozole and drank tequila, and talked, laughed, flirted, in a garden with a giant striped cactus and apricot trees, hidden from the street behind adobe walls.

Within a few hours of this town, founded by the conquistadores – and a few hours travel is nothing in Mexico – I could arrive in tropical rainforest, walk through pines and oaks in temperate highlands, or climb among ferns and bromeliads in the mountain cloud forest. And I needed to speak Spanish well in order to learn the names of plants and trees.

Na Bolom, meaning The House of the Jaguar, combines the names of the founders, Frans and Trudi Blom, and balom, the word for jaguar in the local Mayan language, Tzotzil. The Bloms, a Danish archaeologist and a Swiss photographer, met in Mexico in the late 1930s and soon Trudi was accompanying Frans on his many expeditions on horseback into the Lacandon rainforest.

The great Mayan archaeological sites have frescoes of lords clothed in jaguar skins, and carvings of jaguars guard the temples. The animal sacred to the Maya has become a symbol of the wilderness it needs in order to survive. It was the Bloms' friendship with the indigenous people of the Lacandon that made them aware of the fragile balance of people and forest.

In particular, it was Trudy's friendship with Chan Kin Viejo, eloquent elder spokesman for the forest people, that convinced the Bloms to make their home a centre to show the relationship of Maya past and present with the land. As Chan Kin Viejo is quoted as saying, 'Every time a tree is cut down, a star falls from the sky.' A memorable way of pointing out our effect on the the world around us.

On my first visit to Chiapas in 1993, I had met Lacandon people, who call themselves *hach winik*, the true people, at Palenque, an archaeological site reclaimed from the rainforest and still surrounded by enormous buttressed trees and cinnamon scented vines. Distinctive among the brilliant colours of souvenir stalls in their white cotton shifts with long black hair, wispy beards and with a jokey intelligent self confidence, Lacandon men sold sets of bows and arrows to tourists outside the palace and temples of their ancestors.

At Na Bolom, Frans and Trudy provided friendship, lodging and campaigning support for highland villages, as well as the Lacandon but Trudy's long collaboration with Chan Kin Viejo made a unique bond with the *hach winik*. She lived to the age of 94, surviving Frans by 30 years, and Chan Kin Viejo achieved an extraordinary 101 years. Na Bolom continues this bond, providing free lodging for Lacandon families on visits to San Cristobal. It also provides a library, a museum and a photographic archive for academics and researchers, anthropologists and archaeologists, in the belief that knowledge of the rainforest and the way of life of its inhabitants is valuable for everyone.

Current information from Na Bolom told me that volunteers would need fluent Spanish, a specialist degree and be able to stay for at least 18 months. The exception was for those who wanted to work in the garden. I looked at photographs of lilies shaded by cypress and oaks, the rows of vegetables, and read that garden volunteers did not need fluent Spanish and would be welcome for six months plus.

Later, when I was settled in at Na Bolom, I saw that the volunteer programme had been more or less discontinued and yet every day brought several email enquiries. Then I realised how easily, how fortuitously, I had arrived.

hul
arrival

CHAPTER 1

At the House of the Jaguar

'I am going to capture a soul, now, gods of the earth,
and our mothers of the earth, here, today, now, this soul.'

MAYAN INVOCATION

Black rosettes on a tawny coat, each rosette with its own black spot, the jaguar's beautiful and subtle patterns merge easily into the forest, a forest of green palms, thick grey trunks with deep buttresses, the bleeding red bark of tropical birch, brown leaf mulch. Big and heavy headed, named *yaguar* in the Mayan language meaning one who kills in a single bound, the jaguar is lord of the night, the sun god who goes to the underworld at sunset, a symbol of transformation.

At night or in the early dawn, he slides out of bamboo undergrowth or from a cave dug under a rock and pads along the paths of his territory, a seven foot length of muscled weight, tail carried low in a shallow curve. The forest he walks is his garden, a living food store bounded by scraped trunks and the acrid scent of his urine markers. Alone, for the jaguar is a solitary creature, he follows the peccary, fierce wild pig foraging in groups, smelling the trail of snouts rooting for acorns, or the odour of fresh droppings.

The peccary hasn't a chance, three hundred pounds of mature beast, the jaguar leaps crushing the skull in one movement of the great canine teeth. He pulls the carcass into a tangled mass of young trees and vines and in seclusion eats, tearing and masticating flesh and bone working from the opened head down.

A river never far away, the jaguar swims well, alert and swift enough to catch fish, strong enough to kill and carry a caiman across the wide stretch of water, or shatter the shell of a river turtle for the soft nutritious meat.

Power, skill and beauty were the desirable qualities the Mayan rulers drew into themselves from this creature who is so perfectly suited to the forest. Above all, the jaguar was prized as a symbol of transformation. Elusive and functioning in the dark at the time human beings dream, the body dormant and the mind or soul acting freely, the jaguar represented the visionary in man. Instinct led me to the place named for him, Na Bolom, House of the Jaguar, and the forest which inspired that place, the Lacandon.

The coach took two hours to wind its heavy way round the tight mountain curves up to San Cristobal de Las Casas. Stuck behind trucks with tyres bigger than people and solid wave high bumpers, every car and packed minivan overtook us. And from my elevated seat some of the biodiversity I had read so much about flew by, orange breasted birds, families of parrots, vultures and whirring black creatures like toy helicopters.

On my right side the mountain dropped to the humid plains and Tuxtla Guttierez, the state capital of Chiapas in southern Mexico, where I had arrived by plane from Mexico City. If I looked up on my left, I saw impossible slopes littered with felled tree trunks, the earth burnt and smoking. Black plumes rose over the mountain peaks and narrow valleys, the highest and most inaccessible ranges still thickly forested. Small churches and a few painted tin roofed houses perched on bare lower ridges.

I thought this slash and burn farming was illegal and practised only in the remote forest but here it was, unashamed, along a main road. In England, theories of conservation and ecology, the good and the bad, were clearly defined. In Chiapas I found an issue as hazy and confusing as the smoky landscape unfurling in front of me while the bus travelled higher and higher towards my destination, Na Bolom, and its garden, where I would be working for the next seven months.

San Cristobal emerged above the smoke and traffic, a shining town among mountains with its white houses and orange roofs arranged in neat grids. I looked up towards the zocalo trying to reconcile my memory of it with this reality. The town was busier than I remembered from my previous visit ten years earlier. The graffiti on the broad church wall had changed from protest against homegrown Mexican military to anger against the U.S. The invasion of Iraq was under way.

I needed to pause before reacquainting myself with this place, founded by the Spanish conquerors and commemorating the name of a defender of Indian rights, Fray Bartolomé de las Casas. And I needed to pause before presenting myself at Na Bolom. So I pulled my case along the narrow streets to a pension, optimistically named Casa Real, the Royal House. Falling onto the king size bed, I slept after my marathon journey from the flat lands of Suffolk to the highlands of Chiapas.

I woke to a king size storm. A power cut made a black out setting as shafts of lightning competed with rolls of thunder and the thrum of torrential rain. My room was built against a wall surrounding a flat roof, and I opened the door and returned to bed where tucked under warm blankets, I enjoyed the spectacle. The banana tree from the courtyard below arched against the pantiled roofs of the town and every lightning flash lit up its broad leaves.

The display over, I went out to eat, mindful of the six hour time change and the necessity of adapting. Storm water poured down the street towards the central plaza, and I saw why the pavements were a foot high. Under the arches of the plaza, men held up rain capes for sale, a sign that this was not a one off event even though the rainy season proper wasn't due for another two months or more.

Storms accompanied all my travels in Mexico. One became a hurricane. It was August, the summer of 1993, and my first visit to Mexico. My friends had gone home leaving me on the beach at Tulum with a book, The Hundred Year Mayan War. In between swims and meals I read about survivors of the Spanish invasion hidden in the jungle, protected by sacred crosses and a belief in invincible spiritual powers. Carlos, the patron of the tiny holiday retreat, promised a meeting with a man who knew everything about this Mayan history.

Pablo Canche turned up one afternoon as I sat on the sand between black rocks, and shared a coconut, the juice laced with rum. While the iguanas baked in the sun nearby, spiked profiles raised like a personal armed guard, Pablo Canche explained, 'the war is still on. Not one hundred years, more! Maya still resist. Like me. Look at me and look at Carlos and Paulo.'

I looked at him. A small brown man, muscled from fishing and handling boats every day. And I thought of Carlos and Paulo, plump and smooth, men from the city hanging out on the coast with their tasteful beach hut business. We drank to Mayan resistance.

'You read your book, and understand. Better you read Maya people and understand more.' And Pablo cracked the shell on a rock and left me with a shard of white coconut meat.

The next day the hurricane hit. It began with steady rain. Bored and captive I read and lay on the bed in my thatched hut until hunger for grilled meat, mangoes and coffee roused me. My window was a square cut in the bamboo stick wall and the pangs of my stomach turned from hunger to fear when I saw palm trees bent at right angles and rain speeding in horizontal gusts obliterating the line between land and sea. As I pushed the door it smacked against the bamboo wall and in a whirling second my hair and dress moulded wetly to me. Where was everyone? The owners? the Spaniards in the next hut? Was I forgotten?

A truck drew in and police in black storm gear shouted, 'You must leave the coast, go to the village school, everyone must leave. Now,' and they ran to warn Carlos and Paulo who appeared on their verandah. I was indeed the only remaining guest and they gathered me, blankets and beer, and we drove away from the eye of the hurricane sweeping down the coast towards Tulum.

It was a noisy stay in a crowded school hall. By midnight the wind diminished, and Carlos said, 'Vamonos, let's go, it can't be as bad as this.' But on our return we found sodden and smelly huts and for days the sea remained a nasty metallic hue. As the floods seeped away and roads became usable, I took the bus for the mountains of Chiapas and the centre of Mayan life. By chance, I found my way to Na Bolom where what I saw and heard there must have crept into my memory along with Pablo Canche's words until I was free to return all these years later.

This storm that welcomed me back to the Mayan world crashed into San Cristobal in March, well before the hurricane season, but was dramatic enough to remind me that in Mexico, nature is never only a background.

Na Bolom was on the outskirts of town, and I walked, glad to get a feel of this place before I met the people I would work with for the next seven months. Terraces of one storey houses and front room shops sloped upwards, pointed mountains made a jagged edge to this place, a bowl almost 3,000 metres above sea level. Indian women sat on corners with heaps of peanuts and pyramids of avocados. Parrot screeches issued through the iron curlicues of windows. Chicken legs smoked on charcoal street grills. Town streets where Spanish Mexican and local Maya lived their parallel lives. Among those sharp highlands overlooking the town, it was all Maya; Tzotzil or Tzeltal, Chol or Tojolobal.

The cobbled street ended at dark red walls and a man at the open door of a larger and grander colonial building, Na Bolom. He directed me to a passageway between two courtyards where I found Fabiola Sanchez, Na Bolom's director, in her office. I couldn't quite believe all my planning had translated into that moment of arrival and that Fabiola was welcoming me, the expected volunteer.

'Get a taxi to bring your luggage, here's some money, and stay here until you feel settled. Elisa will show you which room.'

Elisa Maria, the name on the friendly emails over the last months, turned out to be a chica in jeans with long honey blonde hair and dark eyes, younger and hipper than I expected. The arrangement was garden work in exchange for breakfast and supper but not lodging. Elisa's emails had assured me of help to find a place to live, and how cheap and simple this was. But this temporary room offered an easy entry into the new life, I was very happy to stay here while I found my place in it.

'Your room. You like it?' Elisa said, opening the wooden shutters and uncovering a green view into the garden. 'This was Frans Blom's room, Trudy's room is next door, much bigger, she had more clothes.' And she laughed.

Frans Blom's room was small with a tiled floor, dark oak window and door and a brick fireplace, the hearth ready with a bundle of kindling and a stack of logs. A row of well used books lined up on the bedside table, and the bed looked monastically narrow. Elisa patted the thick blankets, 'You have been in San Cristobal before? You will like these blankets tonight,' she admonished, seeing my unenthusiastic look.

It was a plain room for essential needs, shaded by plants outside the one window, a room for a single person, Frans Blom, and now me.

'Look, you can wash here,' and Elisa opened a door and revealed a bath, deep and narrow in a tiled room.

'We have something in common, Frans Blom and me,' I said, imagining the heaven of steeping in a hot bath after work.

'A European bath,' she said, as if this was a backward method of cleansing. 'We prefer showers, and temazcal, the steam bath.'

Work, bath, fire, and a room belonging to one of the founders of Na Bolom. Elisa took the bag from my hand and left it on the bed in my new room.

'Come, I will show you everything, Bernardina.' And she led me on a tour.

My room was on one side of the large main courtyard. At every step there was something to look at; prints from the archive of Trudy Blom's photographs lined the walls, doors opened into rooms of artefacts from Frans Blom's archaeological expeditions. Distracted by plants, I paused by the sheep's tail sedum hanging from pots and the orange flowering vines twined round the verandah columns. I wanted to know more of Elisa too.

'What do you do at Na Bolom?' I asked.

'I come to Na Bolom because I am a photographer, like Trudy. That is my real life, to make pictures of people's lives. But my work here is I go to the doctor or hospital with people from the Lacandon or from the mountains. Maybe they don't speak Spanish so well or they don't trust people. And I make sure they get good treatment.'

And I was sure she did.

'I go to the Lacandon too, that's the forest, to see if someone is fine. You want to come with me sometime? I will ask Fabiola.'

'Yes, I want to.' I said, ready for everything.

'Now you must meet the cook. Very important.'

And she whisked me into the most enormous kitchen I've ever seen, high ceilinged and cool. Elisa told the cook and her companions to provide tea and coffee whenever I pleased. I spoke my careful Spanish and they seemed to understand.

'And here's where you have breakfast and supper,' she said as we entered a long thin room with doors onto each of the two courtyards. A table stretched almost the length of the room, a large ceramic jaguar snarled from a black wooden chest, a paper dragon hung from the ceiling and a tapestry of an elaborately dressed Mayan lord draped the end wall.

'Trudy had so many admirers, always giving her presents,' Elisa explained seeing me attempt to examine at everything.

Na Bolom, like all the colonial buildings was shaped to guard against fierce summer sun in the dry months and downpours of the rainy season. The rooms were protected by the verandah roof that ran inside the main courtyard. Each room was shaded in a permanent mild twilight, heat rising to a tall ceiling, yet here too I noticed a comforting fireplace for chilly highland evenings.

'Every day people come to eat. Sometimes they are staying in the guest rooms or they are friends of Na Bolom, or families from the forest. Everyone eats together. Just say to the kitchen if you want to take supper that evening.'

Spanish and food, a slow taking in together, arranging my thoughts in new words while I tasted new flavours.

As Elisa took me from room to room, dark wood and red or yellow ochre walls were everywhere, the same lime wash colours and oak beams I knew in Suffolk. Here each room opened onto a colonnaded walk around one of the four courtyards, a bougainvillea clung in great swathes to a tree and a pair of hummingbirds darted around its pink purple flowers.

'You want anything, come and find me. I can help you,' Elisa told me and she returned to Fabiola's office.

What I wanted was to meet my place of work. Where was the garden and who was the gardener? Elisa left me as I searched for the words in Spanish.

So before I went to collect my luggage, I found my way through the courts and connecting rooms to an ironwork gate and into the garden. A garden of stepped terraces full of luxuriant growth, rows of white trumpet shaped lilies, blue agapanthus, red and pink geraniums. In among these familiar flowers grew a multitude of unknown plants, all overshadowed by mature pines and oaks, and crossed by winding paths.

Paths led me to guest rooms and the archive of Trudy Blom's photographs, all built against the garden walls and obscured by the tangle of growth. Paths led me to the toolshed and a workshop where a man planed lengths of wood. I passed vegetable beds and aloe vera cacti, and smiled at a woman in a blue overall hanging out laundry. This path ended at a stick hut with palm thatch, the ubiquitous gardener's shed.

A man hurried along, a mug of coffee in one hand, he waved. 'Ian,' he said, stopping, 'It's alright I speak English. You must be the new person, excuse me I'm pretty busy.'

However, he stayed long enough to tell me how he arrived as a volunteer, seven years ago from Canada, stayed and married Fabiola. If Elisa was a Mexio City girl brimming with energy, Ian was quiet and preoccupied, as befits an archivist and chief administrator. It was clear he was available if I really needed him, but that he preferred seclusion in his office or the dark room.

'What sort of hours do people work in the garden?' I asked, still unsure who my colleagues would be.

'from seven to three,' he said, but then went on to suggest various places I might want to visit; the Ecosur library, the Museum of Mayan Medicine.

I felt he didn't assume I would appear at seven in the morning. I'm not good at seven o'clock. And breakfast, part of my volunteer recompense, didn't start until eight.

'And who is the gardener?'

'Manvel, who is away fulfilling his cargo responsibilities,' Ian explained. 'It's very important, an honour and a religious task.' he went on, 'We don't know what Manvel's cargo is. But usually it's looking after the saintsin the village churches, paying for their new clothes, or decorati o ns and for the various ceremonies and fiestas through a whole year.'

Cargo meant carry as in carry responsibility and sounded an expensive burden. I knew from my first visit to Chiapas that in Manvel's village Catholicism was melded with older beliefs and practices that involved drinking enough pox, home distilled spirit, to open the mind to the spiritual world. The world where the saints, the earth lord, the demons live and where every human soul's animal spirit companion is corralled each night. Without pox how can the cargo holders be alert to the needs of their saintly guardians. So my job would be assisting this man who served saints and was familiar with spirits.

As we stood talking, others came along the path. I was introduced to Humberto, who split kindling and replenished the wood supply for every guest room fireplace. And then came Liliana looking for carrots, she orders supplies for the kitchen, and Pepe, the guide who relates the history and ethos of Na Bolom and its founders to visitors. This gentle scrutiny revived me.

'And is it just Manvel who looks after the garden?' I asked hopefully.

'Well, there is Doña Bety,' said Ian. 'You'll come across her.' And he turned, cooling coffee in hand, and disappeared behind the lilac blue blossoms of a jacaranda into a door in the far wall.

Doña Bety. Yet another courtyard, small and crowded with oleander and cacti, led to the library, one path straight through to an open door. I looked for the annual report, as Fabiola suggested, to see who and what were part of Na Bolom, and sat at a table and read. Doña Bety's name headed the list of trustees, former companion, assistant and friend, to Trudy Blom, it said, and the remaining link with the founders of Na Bolom. Doña Bety knew why Frans and Trudy felt so passionately about the forests of Chiapas. She knew why Trudy believed the garden was as much part of the ethos of Na Bolom as the forest. But Doña Bety was not there either.

Properly arrived at Na Bolom, luggage unpacked, I sat in Frans Blom's room writing on the pristine first pages of my journal. Dark wood and firelight made a tranquil and meditative atmosphere, and I left the door open the better to hear someone playing Bach on a grand piano. It must have been like this for Frans Blom back from an archaeological expedition on pack horse or at the end of a day writing up his discoveries in the library. Na Bolom was built as a friars' seminary but never occupied instead it became a grand home for a well off land owning family. The private chapel remained. Statues of saints and ceilings painted with cherubs showed its original purpose and it was from the chapel that the music came. Reflection was a built in quality, holding the history of this place.

Above San Cristobal firecrackers ripped into the night sky. No cascades of light poured down, just almighty bangs punctuating the obsessive variations of the piano. It must be a feast day tomorrow.

CHAPTER 2

A Gardener of Substance

My quest to become a gardener of substance began. I called it a quest because now I was here I wasn't so sure of myself. Was I too fixed in my habits? Would I be able to use the knowledge I did have? Would the gardeners, the real gardeners, appear and show me better ways than my haphazard methods? Was I too old after all to work consistently six or seven hours a day, five days a week, for months. This was hard for me to admit to myself, I hadn't even considered it before I arrived, as usual gaily convinced that determination meant capability.

After several days I still got lost in the garden, wondering which path to go along to find the bed I was working on before, surprised where the path led. There were a dozen ways to reach the compost area behind the hedge and I could never work out which was the least winding and bumpy for the wheelbarrow. The garden overwhelmed me, I loved it's easy growth, its cluttered beauty, the hidden places I was still finding. And I loved what I met there, sudden scents, a twisted cactus, a wedge tailed bird whose feathers gleamed like spilt petrol.

In the mornings, I hesitated unsure whether to work on the vegetable beds or clear the pine needles from among the thick lily leaves. A clear perspective of the garden geography and my role within it eluded me. I hoped Manvel would return soon. Adding to my confusion Ian walked by each morning and said, 'and the orchids need organising,' waving a hand at a cascade of white blooms tied to a tree with blue plastic twine, 'and those really need some attention. Find out what they're called.' Or he pointed out all the things that dismayed him and that I didn't notice at all, a damaged path edge, bits of plastic and other debris clotting the earth, the lack of plants in such and such a bed.

By midday the heat became intense. I was determined to prove my worth, but however vigorously I dug and hoed and forked and left each day sweaty with effort, the garden resisted transformation. I couldn't see that I had done anything in particular. But what I saw and what others saw was quite different.

The one path I got to know well was the one set with stones, a roughly cobbled path, which led up to a couple of office rooms and the guest rooms. On this path, Lacandon families from the rainforest, visitors and Fidelia, the friendly laundress, all walked past and complimented me on the loveliness of the garden, encouraging me in my impossible task. The visitors probably believed I actually was capable of all this as if the garden was an expression of my will. But I couldn't respond quickly enough in Spanish to voice my reservations, to be English and deny responsibility for this beauty.

Doña Bety remained elusive. A small soft voiced woman in her seventies, her house was in the opposite corner to Manvel's shed. I expected to work alongside her or at her instruction, but when I introduced myself she looked up at me with her remarkable blue ringed brown eyes and said, 'I'll be here later and then we can do something together.'

I watched her short round figure in navy trousers and grey jumper go through the arch that led to the outside world, but she didn't return. I looked for her again in those first weeks but we never quite coincided. Those magical eyes held my attention each time she offered a pleasant explanation of why we couldn't garden together right then. It was only when I met someone else with the same combination that I found out those blue ringed irises were a sign of high cholesterol.

Since neither of the two gardeners, Manvel and Doña Bety, were around, one busy with the saints in his village, Chamula, the other apparently unavailable, I was on my own. I fixed on two beds, the medicine and the dye plants, and decided to give these my attention, forking and adding sieved compost, even thinking to expand the range of sample plants. Both were on the guided tour that Pepe gave.

Pepe, whose Tzeltal Indian family came from the far side of those volcanic mountains, hid behind dark shades and a pirate headscarf. Every day at 11.30 I watched him entertain a cluster of strangers, and his tours were performance art, wonderfully exaggerated anecdotes laced with jokes. But also as informative for me as for the visitors. I sat back on my heels and listened.

'Frans liked to be known as Don Pancho. He was a self educated academic and liked to play the brave adventurer, a monteador, and made light of his disappointments, his failure to discover significant ancient Mayan remains. He came close to, but missed, two extraordinary places; Bonampak's frescoes, the only frescoes with the colours still vivid and the figures clear, and the most impressive of all Maya burial chambers, the Lord Pakal's tomb at Palenque. Every archaeologist's dream. Can you imagine the bitterness of that? No wonder he drank.

And no man likes to be upstaged by his wife, a much younger wife. You saw Trudy's splendid collection of jewellery, showy, flamboyant. That was her!'

As the visitors were ushered on to admire the tree nursery saplings, Pepe talked about the Blom's friendship with the present day Maya.

'Frans had the guts to listen to his wife though. While he looked for ruins, she made friends with the living descendants of the Maya, forest people like Chan Kin Viejo, and this friendship made them determined to replant and protect the forests.'

At times I moved along behind Pepe's group, weeding in their footsteps so I could hear the next part of his story. The serious information was livened up with stories about the formidable Trudy. And this was Trudy's garden after all. She planted this garden according to organic principles, using compost to enrich the soil and trees to shade seedlings.

Pepe had his party pieces too, squeezing the berries of pitz'otz to demonstrate the colour and explaining that this, with clay as a fixative, was used to dye the black woollen skirts worn by Chamulan women. The first time I watched him in action I saw that the juice itself was purple and heard it made black but the plant label said pitz'otz made green. Pepe would scorn labels but I seized on it as something I could do, correct the label.

His next stop was the nearby bed where a statue of Diego Rivera, the Mexican muralist, bottle and book in hand, stood among rose bushes, several women clinging to him. Soon I heard the joking remarks about his talents, artistic and seductive, so often I could repeat them in Spanish as well as English from the two daily tours. I felt the artist's serious work was ignored in favour of amusing visitors and decided to redress this.

Diego Rivera painted the flower growers and the flowers, the most famous an Indian woman bearing on her back a great basket of calla lilies. He deserved a bed of flowers of his own, a bed of adoring flowery devotees. I made it my homage to keep this plot weed free with blooms dead headed, to cultivate a thick cluster of plants around Diego's pedestal. It became one of my chosen jobs to transplant the rogue seedlings that sprang up so freely in the warm damp earth to grow at his feet.

Most afternoons, work finished, I sank into the bath. It was a good thinking place, especially with a beer and one of those forbidden treats, a cigarette. Refreshed, I set off into town to try out some new activity like finding the main post office or having a coffee somewhere, returning to eat supper with the evening's guests at the long table.

English and Spanish were used as lingua franca interwoven with Maya, German, Dutch and French. Guests were agronomists, linguists, Phd students on research grants, and travellers enthusiastic about the history, the cultures of Chiapas and its range of landscapes, from mountain villages to tropical valleys. Almost every night guests included families up from the rainforest communities of Lacanha, Naha or Metza Bok for medical appointments arranged by Elisa or to sell sets of bow and arrows in the market around Santo Domingo church.

Each night brought a surprise group of dining companions. It was impossible not to talk to my neighbours as I passed at least six laden dishes down the table one after the other; fried plaintain, chicken in a delicious savoury chocolate sauce, chayote, a sort of squash layered with white cheese, huge bowls of salad. How could I be lonely when this instant dinner party was here every night. But in between I wondered about my work in the garden, about the people I was supposed to be working with, felt a flutter of homesickness.

It was a small dinner group and I turned to speak to the elderly Lacandon couple on my left. Kayum Maax and his wife Chanakin were from Lacanha, each had long hair still shining black, they wore shin length tunics, hers a floral red and purple, his white. In a few minutes we were all talking together, deep in a real conversation.

'I used to live here at Na Bolom, when Trudy was alive.' Kayum Maax told me, 'Did they tell you about me? I was like her son, you know. But some people, they don't want that. Trudy was strict! Yes, it was a whack with her stick if she saw elbows on the table, anyone, not only me, and adults not just children. If she didn't like someone, she could be rude, shout or ignore them. And it didn't matter who was here, all kinds of people came to see Trudy, important people too from Mexico City and from Europe.

If you see a photograph, two boys on a horse, then that's me with my brother. It was taken in the forest, before I lived here, one that Trudy took many years ago.'

Before coffee arrived, I looked for the photograph Kayum Maax described and there it was in the corridor just by Fabiola's office door, two small boys in white tunics and wide brimmed straw hats. They sat on a horse or perhaps one of the pack mules belonging to the Bloms, one behind the other, two pale human shapes surrounded by the dense foliage of the forest. I imagined Trudy posing them, teasing them and making them laugh before they settled serious and still for the time it took an old fashioned camera to record.

'That's where I will take you, Bernardina. That is the Lacandon,' a now familiar voice said.

'Why are you still here, Elisa?'

'I use the darkroom sometimes. You know who that is? Did you talk with him?'

'Kayum Maax. Yes, he told me about Trudy, that he used to live here.'

'His parents died. But can you imagine? Trudy for a mother? She was a brave woman but not a mother, she sent him away to boarding school, a good school, she wanted Kayum Maax to grow up and be like Chan Kin Viejo, and speak for the community.'

'Hard to imagine that little boy in a boarding school. So what happened?'

'What do you think? He ran away. It was not an easy life for a Lacandon boy. Not easy for him to be what Trudy hoped. Now I must go because Cesar is waiting for me.' She smiled and waved to a figure leaning against the far wall by the entrance where Carlos, the doorman stood. Carlos, always ready to greet but whose disconcertingly small presence would never deter any unwelcome visitor.

I returned to the dining table and Kayum Maax and Chanakin smiled, patting my arms, satisfied that I had identified that child. From that moment the photos hanging in rows along the passage walls and in every room, some of the thousands of photographs taken by Trudy Blom over the decades of her long life in Chiapas, began to tell me about the lives of the people in them. When I met Lacandon families next at meals or on the garden path, I scanned older faces for their earlier selves who I might see in the black and white prints.

From Pepe, Elisa, Fidelia and others, I began to fit little bits of information together about Trudy, her long life after Frans' death, how she took responsibility for the young Kayum. I began to understand that she wanted to make certain someone could act as a bridge between the people of the rainforest and the modern world when Chan Kin Viejo died.

Kayum Maax disappointed Trudy by abandoning the forest gods, and converting to the protestant beliefs of the school. But in spite of his new beliefs, he ran away from the mission school and returned to the Lacandon. But all this I understood later, that evening I listened.

CHAPTER 3

Allies and Obstacles

'weeds do not have good souls,
they are like people who pay no attention'

FROM THE MAYA

One morning as Fidelia pegged sheets on the laundry terrace, a man walked out of the stick and thatch shed beyond. Manvel. The gardener's shed was open again, and a bike leant against a peach tree. Shed, bike, and I found that he shared another universal gardener's characteristic; the solitary worker's reluctance to talk. We shook hands and had the first of our many conversations of few words. I spoke and he nodded staring down at the carrot seedlings as if they had an urgent need of him after his attention to other worlds. Mattock in hand, he simply waited until my questions failed and I fell back on suggesting my own next job, to which he nodded agreeably.

However, I wasn't ready to let him go. Hoping I would understand my place in the garden now that the gardener had returned I waited as if for some revelation. Perhaps Manvel himself wasn't ready to settle back into his usual routine, and so we walked the paths and paused by this vegetable bed or that patch of flowers. No explanations were offered but as he stood there, I supplied the words like a commentary. 'The beetroot are almost ready to eat,' or ' these look a bit crowded'.

On that first day I followed him and stood there in that curious way of getting to know each other until he decided to continue his day and began to turn the earth between the rows of feathery carrot tops. The mattock came down easily and the loamy earth, still damp rose dark and almost edible to look at, like crumbled cooking chocolate. Content with this minimal introduction, I left Manvel and set about my own day, taking a hand fork and transplanting spinach seedlings to a sparsely filled bed.

After this, Manvel got on with his work each day and behaved in a tolerant way towards this keen foreigner. In spite of this lack of guidance, I attempted to be his assistant. I needed a *jefe*, a boss, someone at least to tell what I've done. As if by saying it aloud, the work itself was fixed, the weeding stay weeded, the transplants thrived, the pine cones refrained from falling on the herb bed.

Every morning I searched the garden until I found him, 'What shall I do today, Manvel?' He thought up some trifling task for me, I did it and felt good, then moved on to whatever impossible project I took upon myself. I didn't understand yet that no one expected to me to work alongside them, which was still what I craved to do.

For Manvel everything here was self - evident. My keenness to find out, to be told, bemused him. When I mentioned something to Felicia about Manvel knowing this garden so well, she shouted over to him, 'How long have you been here?' then, 'And how old are you, Manvel?' which seemed excessively frank but was answered without hesitation. 'There you are,' she said, always ready for conversations, repeating, 'He's worked at Na Bolom since he was thirteen, more than forty years,' adding, 'And his father, Juanito, was here before that.'

Once coming from the back office where Liliana, Marie and Romero, entertained me with gossip and themselves with me, I met an old man in leather sandals and straw hat carrying a bunch of agapanthus the size of a sheaf of corn. This was Manvel's father, still growing plants aged 83, just arriving a little later in the day than his son, to sell his flowers in the market.

Manvel's family lived in one of the hamlets, a scattered arrangement of houses within the larger parish known as Chamula. He cycled down from his mountain home to San Cristobal, rising in the dark in order to arrive at seven am, I knew it was still dark at six. I don't like asking questions and yet conversation with this amiable man didn't develop unless I found some not too foolish enquiry. But I waited until I felt at home in his territory and we had developed a working friendliness where he came and leant on his mattock somewhere nearby. I took this as a sign, a wordless invitation, for me at least to speak.

If I didn't feel obliged to talk enough for both of us, he would offer the sort of easy query like any agricultural worker in Suffolk might, an opening to slowly gather morsels to ponder the rest of the day. 'Is it the rainy season in your country?' or 'how much maize grows in England?'

Eventually I grew bolder, keen to hear about his life. 'So you're a cargo holder?' But however much I tried, he acknowledged my interest politely and that was it. 'Yes, a big responsibility.'

As we did come to know each other, I asked more pertinent questions, 'Why has the compost got so many pine needles in?'

'It's organic, organic is very good. Everything here is organic.' And with sufficient to think about for a while, he sloped off to accomplish great swathes of hoeing with his mattock or have a plot seeded with the next carrot crop before once again merging into the garden background.

All gardeners in San Cristobal seemed to come from Chamula. All houses had a garden, often secreted away. Walking down Calle Tapachula in the cool evenings, I passed the courtyard garden where a large family ate supper, a metal gate open to the street. Neighbour's children sat on the step. The courtyard had a tree, a central flowerbed and a clutter of potted plants. There were homes with walls and heavy wooden doors, and it was impossible to tell that behind these were gardens, with grass, vines, fruit trees, gardens only glimpsed as someone entered or left. Men came down from Chamula to spend a day skillfully cutting grass with a machete, use the ubiquitous mattock, and move from one garden to another, one for each day through the week.

There was another highland parish with a particular affinity with plants, Zinacantan, Chamula's neighbouring, and historically rival, parish. Zinacantecos never worked in anything so small as a garden, they cultivated flowers on a grander, commercial scale, and they dressed to match their trade. I saw them in town and sometimes took the minibus to their market up in the mountains. Zinacanteco men wore tunics embroidered with sunflowers, huge bunches of flowers, life size baskets of flowers, decorated with glittering metallic thread on hot pink or pine green cloth. The women wore short embroidered shawls in the same colours and style.

Fields of carnations and chrysanthemums surrounded the central village of Zinacantan like a floral stockade. The blooms were sold to Tuxtla and even Mexico City, pre hispanic home of the flower gardens of the Aztec nobles, gardens whose splendour astonished the Spanish invaders.

Chamulan men tended the flowers in ladino gardens, ladino, town dwelling descendants of Spanish colonists and the indigenous people. Chamulan wear tends to be darker than their neighbours, blue and black are their colours, indicating their more reserved character and serious even fearsome, reputation. Manvel certainly upheld the reserved part of this reputation.

Manvel completed the team of outdoor workers at Na Bolom. I had met Humberto on my first day, and at night enjoyed lighting the wood he left so neatly by the fireplace in Frans Blom's room. Javier, guardian of tools and head of everything outside was responsible for an extraordinary range of maintenance. I saw him redo a bathroom, block up doors and open new windows, build whole guest rooms against the garden wall complete with plumbing, wiring and built in cupboards.

When this modest miracle worker handed me a key to the tool shed, I took it as a mark of confidence as well as a practical answer to my morning requests for trowels and rakes. Perhaps he was relieved that I attached myself, however tentatively, to Manvel and could therefore be trusted not to lose tools.

The tool shed cut into the underneath of Doña Bety's house at the far end of the garden. It was cool and dark with pegs and narrow shelves along the wall. Like all tool sheds it had order and jumble, each fork, spade and rake had their place on a peg, and I knew where to find the trowel on the narrow shelf above. Along the opposite side lay a stack of unused plastic pots and useful tubs with dried paint and cobwebs. I learnt how to feel for the hook, reached through a gap above the wooden door, where I left the padlock key at the end of the day.

To the side of the tool shed was the workshop enclosed by a trellis wall. I could see the power tools and lengths of wood waiting for Javier's transforming hand. The workshop was open and busy when I arrived at 8.30 am, long after the men had begun the day.

Since Manvel attended mainly to vegetables and keeping overall order, I liked to pick out a new spot that lay comfortably undisturbed. Often I found plants obscured in a jumble of twigs and dead leaves or overgrown by creepers. A striped cactus, maguey, made babies in hope of survival, the spiny swords poking through the brown and dusty covering. I raked away masses of debris and wheeled it to the constantly smouldering bonfire. Gradually, the earth appeared and made a beautiful rich setting for the green and yellow maguey. The next task was to rearrange or remove the smaller ones and allow the parents to grow and fill the space as a more glorious display.

That was the moment that drew onlookers and comments, the moment I felt like those outdoor painters examining the subject before them as curious passers by looked over their shoulder and made remarks, gave advice or warnings.

And if Elisa wasn't using the darkroom or away making health visits we made arrangements to meet after our workday had ended in Bar Revolucion. Sometimes I saw her early evenings walking in the zocalo, with the young man with long hair and a skimpy Jesus beard. They had an unapproachable togetherness air. I noticed him at Na Bolom waiting around silent and cool quite unlike the cheerful, inquisitive staff, and unlike the Elisa I was getting to know.

Arriving at lunch time to talk and smoke an 'Ala' while I ate my bread and avocado picnic, she apologised for not coming to say hello the previous evening.

'Cesar is going away and he wants to spend every moment together,' she explained, 'I will be sad, I want to go with him but he says this is something he has to do without me.'

This romantic suffering sounded familiar, she at home waiting and he having brave adventures, a familiar story not just in my past but right through history. Hadn't this been rewritten feminist style? However, Cesar did set off, in this case into the Lacandon forest to live with the Maya. Elisa discussed his actions as to motives and susceptibility to her influence and love, while I listened and made as helpful and wise comments as I could. Cesar far away, we spent more evenings at Bar Revolucion.

Elisa was pretty and popular and many handsome young men kept her from suffering unnecessarily. In San Cristobal long hair for men was still the fashion and the thick black locks gave an arty, rebel and manly appearance all at the same time. The nickname for San Cristobal inhabitants is 'coleta', the same word for what we call inelegantly, pigtails, the pigtails the Spanish wore when they founded the town, so maybe long hair for men has never stopped being a proud sign of being a 'coleta'.

Elisa looked confident and assumed everybody was mad about her, and often she was right. But just as she settled down without Cesar, got involved in her work, in photography projects, with evenings at Bar

Revolucion talking rebel politics or considering her own craving to run off and live in the forest, then Cesar reappeared unable to keep up the revolutionary hero life after all. He didn't stay long, just long enough to unsettle Elisa and remind her that he was the one she wanted.

Her spell embraced everyone else. I felt warmed and softened by her optimism, her cheerful and volatile belief in justice, by her direct way of getting in close to the people she liked or worked with. When we walked in the cathedral plaza children came and hung onto Elisa, she talked to them, played with them. When Enrique brought his wife for advice about mysterious stomach pains, she helped them persevere through the bureaucracy of forms and tests and results. At times she had to make difficult decisions.

As I passed by reception one morning, a thin man in a suit sat there head bent, resisting advice from the entire admin staff, Auracelie and Liliana and Marie.

'Hospital is the best place.'

'The nurses will look after you there.'

'They have the proper medicines.'

His daughter held a small child and looked harassed and said. 'I have to go back today. I can't stay any longer.'

Elisa arrived and the man looked at her. His face was grey.

'I'm alone in hospital. Help me go home to Lacanha.'

Yes, I think, why die comfortably but far away from your family. Elisa knelt by his chair and people left to get on with their work. 'We'll find a place for you in the van. Carlos is going to the Lacandon tomorrow.'

The pattern of my day settled. I began with a sustaining breakfast, eggs scrambled with red pepper and onion, beans mashed up like brown potato, tortillas, and coffee, served by sulky Angel the morning waiter. Next I went to work in the garden, took a picnic lunch break outside the library chatting with Cecilia, the librarian, and had supper with a procession of interesting guests. Elisa became my link, and often my interpreter, with this new life, appearing in the garden or at the open door of Frans Blom's room. My temporary room was always his room and I was the invited and welcome guest, if still an outsider in the garden.

And most evenings there was some social event; a film club showing, an exhibition opening. Or I enjoyed coffee and conversation with friends in the walkway by the zocalo, and watched the Chiapaneco world, the children from the village communities selling painted clay animals, the mothers with babies at the breast sitting on pavements steps making woven belts or embroidering blouses, Tzotzil men selling sweets and cigarettes from a set of miniature shelves on their chests.

People crowded the streets like Victorian photographs, talking or leaning indolent against shop doorways. There were affectionate greetings between families. Men in plastic cowboy hats and woven tunics stood on the corner of Avenida General Utrillo, moustachioed business men sat with a newspaper, one foot on a shoe shine stool. If I sat there for an hour outside Cafe Aroma with my cup of local coffee, I would soon be talking to Fredy, who refused to speak English to foreigners, Adriana who ran the children's ecology workshops for Na Bolom, Megan, the American archaeologist who researched her PhD in Na Bolom's library, Cristina, the guide who spoke six languages. The world met here.

It took fifteen minutes to walk home through my favourite streets. I went up Calle Comitan past the church of Barrio Cerillo with its anti politician graffiti, past the pink house with the old man and his parrot, the bright green house where if I was lucky, a boy lounged on the window ledge playing guitar.

Turning into cobbled Calle Tapachula, there was the corner house where visiting academics stayed, the big palm rising above the roof and at the end of this narrow street, the red ochre walls of Na Bolom. I said goodnight to Carlos, guardian and van driver, collected my key and crossed the courtyard. Frans Blom's adventures with tropical ticks and wild pigs became my bedtime reading as I listened through my earphones to Sonidos de Amor on Radio San Cristobal.

The garden began to feel a little more welcoming. I thought it would be the perfect place to be, where I offered my amateur experience and learnt from others whose daily life was the garden and the forests. I had imagined, without even being aware of my hopes, that this would be a refuge, an enclosed retreat where the hurried untidiness of life was left behind. A homing instinct had led me past all obstacles to the garden of the House of the Jaguar after my 60th birthday and that first reflection on finding a new purpose and new understanding of plants, the cultivated and the wild. I suppose I hoped for a working paradise, and found I hadn't yet earned my place.

My place arrived in small moments, unexpectedly and sometimes unrecognised. 'Bernardine is our volunteer. She will tell you about the garden.' Fabiola, on a rare excursion from the office, plunged me into a fluency I did not suspect. She left after this abrupt introduction, and the small group of visitors watched as I clambered down the bank from cutting back an over boisterous rose. They looked at me, assured that I was a true source of knowledge and my vocabulary responded to their interest.

The couple from Mexico City listened to every word as I talked about the garden, pointing out the bromeliads and wild orchids rescued from forest clearance. I surprised myself as I told their stories, remembering the bromeliad, *tillandsia guatemalensis,* was the same plant that hung over church altars on saints' days. 'From Inglaterra!' they said impressed, 'well, we will have to do our part too, and raise some funds for Na Bolom.'

The Lacandon families continued to encourage me. The men in white tunics and lace up boots, the young wives in ankle length jean skirts, older wives in flowered skirts and short tunics would exclaim. 'It's lovely,' or 'you do work well,' and smiled approvingly.

'My mother used that when we had worms,' Enrique said, pointing to epazote in the herb bed. 'It got rid of loads.' I could imagine. A procession of pregnant women in town for their check ups stopped to smile.

It was at breakfast time that Angel, so provocatively named, reminded me I was still a lowly member of Na Bolom. As each person appeared at the table, Angel placed yoghourt, fruit salad and a glass of fresh orange juice before them. Dressed in formal waiter garb, black trousers and waistcoat, he stood attentively by each guest while they chose their cooked breakfast dish. He smiled at them, with me he reverted to his moody look, those strong features and smoothly gleaming hair daring me to admire and linger. I tried to insist on his attention, calling, 'Angel, por favor, Angel', but he walked away. I had to get up and lean through the serving hatch, 'Milk please, I would like milk for my coffee.'

I was never ready for this first test of resolve. This was the time I felt like one of the street dogs cringing over the compost heap, but confused by such treatment, it upset me far more than seemed fitting. Why should I feel like a fragile child, when I knew myself as a strong grandmother. If I had the confidence and cheekiness of Elisa I would go into the kitchen, which the staff hated, and help myself.

At the end of the day Rogelio, the supper waiter, redeemed my pride. 'Hola, good evening, here, come here!' and he had the chair out ready for me. For Rogelio, I was a bonus diner, delighted to respond to his cheery attempts at English phrases. This was the man my father, guv'nor of a public house with his motto of 'the customer is always right' would have approved of. Rogelio liked to see his customers happy, satisfied with the food, the service, and each other. He laughed at their jokes just like my Dad, he remembered I preferred drinking Sol, just as customers came to The Black Horse because Dad knew whether they liked Worthington E or Guinness, their ham sliced thin or thick and because he listened to them. And although underage, when I stood in at lunchtime in the more select lounge bar the detectives from the local police station forgot that and told me their stories instead.

Some evenings I ate out in town, at El Gato Gordo where I spread the day's newspaper, La Jornada, out beside my plate of grllled meat or matched words and pictures on the television's Chiapas news. But I needed breakfast at Na Bolom, taking the few steps from my room to the dining table every morning at 8 am. Instead of moving slowly from a dream state to alertness to the task at hand, I had to brace myself to overcome the first challenge.

Elisa jumped out of the office as I passed on my way to the garden. She greeted me looking very pleased with herself, 'You're coming to the selva, the rainforest. I told Fabiola you have to come. It's the American college tour. We go in five days to Lacanha. Buy some mosquito repellent.'

I met the Americans at breakfast next morning. 'Don't worry. We're not Bush supporters. Not all of us want war,' said Gordon, joking with a hint of defensiveness. There was no television to watch at Na Bolom, but knowledge of each further 'shock and awe' in Iraq was unavoidable, I saw the newspaper headlines and photographs next to the shoe shine stands in the plaza and once anyone knew I was English they would tell me the day's death toll.

'I believe you,' I said, 'I'm glad I'm here and can't be obsessed with what's going on in Iraq.' I was glad Mexico's constitution forbad war unless attacked, though there were Mexicans who believed that a covert war existed within their own country.

'Here's our cultural studies group. And that's my wife and son.' The son was a typical American boy, large for his nine years, in baggy shorts and baseball cap. And the students, three girls and two boys, all seventeen years old, had an air of not quite believing where they were. I recognised the look, wanted to reassure them.

They acknowledged me from the end of the breakfast table. 'Hi, pleased to meet you,' 'Cool' 'OK!' they said in their polite southern tones.

'And this is my colleague, Greg.' I shook hands with Greg and Greg's companion Jim, muscled and moustached. 'We run the Chiapas trip every year and somehow managed to attract this unlikely and rather innocent group.' Gordon went on, 'We hope if they know nothing then the America further south is bound to be a big discovery.'

Doña Bety passed the open windows, secateurs and basket in hand, and the two professors called her in and presented her to their students, 'Trudy Blom's valued friend and assistant,' and she smiled. I watched the three of them slip into fluent Spanish, old friends, then went out to start my own cultural studies outside.

My command of Spanish was baby talk compared to these professors, and Elisa spoke far too good English for me to dare to put my thoughts into her language. In the Lacandon I would be caught between the temptation to speak English and a determination to keep up with Greg and Gordon. Instead of going straight to work, I took my verb tables and dictionary from the bedside table to revise over lunch.

Before lunch time arrived, I heard, 'Bernardina!' and looked up from my hoeing to see Elisa with a folder in her arms. Sitting at the concrete bench and table under a rose, she laid out her lists of essential supplies for the journey. And while she wrote and crossed out and added up figures, thinking aloud how to fit supplies into the van, I hurried to complete my weed free patch.

'I am ready. We stay at Enrique's, gringos in the visitor cabañas, you and me and Carlos in the storeroom with the sacks.' She laughed. 'Don't worry we have mosquito nets too. And now I get us a drink from the kitchen.' She could prise mugs of coffee out of the kitchen staff. Even Angel didn't resist Elisa's demands.

A journey into La Selva Lacandona, the source of Trudi and Frans Blom's inspiration, the excitement lifted my mind from the garden plants and my silent colleagues. I looked through my clothes for the lightest, coolest, the most suitable for humid forest days and mosquito filled nights. And once there I was determined to set off on my own to find Kayum Maax and Chanakin at home.

'Bernardina, you will love the forest, like me,' Elisa repeated a hundred times. She was right. I wanted to see the ceiba tree rising 50 metres towards the sky, the 'world tree', sacrilegious to fell, and among whose roots Kisin, the Earth Lord lived. He who controlled the elements, the animals and plants.

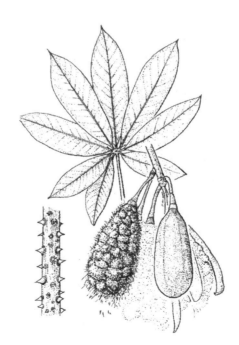

Ceiba pentandra
(ceiba kapok)

CHAPTER 4

Lacanha

Montes Azules, blue mountains. And the haze that blurred their outline
was indeed blue, a soft focus lilac blue from smoke. Most of the giant
mahogany and cedar had been cut and dragged out decades ago and
this fire was burning tracts of secondary growth forest. Mountain
forests on fire not with the small controlled Spring burning on one
family's forest garden, but smoke over large sweeps of land near the
long, straight and empty road, suspiciously convenient for cattle
pasture.

This huge area, almost a million acres, covers mountains, rivers,
lakes and swamps, and rises to over four thousand feet. Montes Azules
includes most of the Lacandon forest and is designated a biosphere.
Sustainable development is permitted, people live here and need to
support themselves. In Na Bolom's shop, incense burners from forest
clay, bark cloth, seed and bowls from the silkily striped wood, jobilla,
provides some with a tiny income. But that is insufficient to halt the
insidious destruction of what could be resources carefully harvested for
human benefit, of habitats preserved for forest creatures.

Butterflies, orchids and birds, I hoped to see some of the hundreds
of varieties there, but 112 mammal species were easily hidden among
the thousands of acres and thousands of plants. The wild pigs, peccaries,
that even the intrepid Frans Blom described as fierce and dangerous,
have disappeared from the trails he travelled. Roads and trucks, our van,
have chased the deer and the jaguar into hidden places.

Despite all the gloomy records, our van became a single small intrusion among the trees as we turned off the smooth highway and drove the rock and earth track to Lacanha and Enrique's hospitality.

Enrique's little granddaughters, Kuti and Margarita ran ahead along the path through their family milpa to the stretch of river for bathing and washing clothes. The milpa was black and grey with the ash of old plants burnt off between banana trees hung with heavy bunches of green fruit. Here in practice, was the idea of forest gardening, the opposite of mono culture. A forest garden is one where a small patch of ground has layers of food plants that help each other. Bananas shade vegetables and chiles, maize gets sun and provides a climbing support for squashes, ash is instant fertilizer.

Stopping to look, I thought of my own garden for the first time, a garden where I tried to keep the rows I had inherited neat with each type of plant in its place, looking proper, orderly and very satisfying in its way. But why did I spend so much energy restraining exuberance and worrying about encroaching plants. Why, if that was when gardening ceased to be a joyous thing. Instinct showed that encouragement and human inconsistency had better results. Sometimes exuberant, sometimes neat rows. Next Spring back in Suffolk I would scatter marigolds alongside the vegetables and let sweet peas trail over the Jerusalem artichokes, morning glory through the fig tree.

'Here! here! Come on,' the girls shouted, pulling off their dresses and leaping into the river. I hung my clothes on a branch and stepped into the clear water. Fast and cold, it rubbed my flesh like an impatient parent as I clung to a log or allowed myself to be rushed to the far end of the pool. Vines hung from trees along the riverbank and as I turned on my back and looked up, a large burgundy coloured butterfly settled on a leaf just above the water. If I stayed drifting like a piece of flotsam, a shoal of tiny fish nibbled my feet and legs in a delicate massage. Kuti and Margarita swam upstream clambering over lime encrusted logs set at intervals across from bank to bank to slow the torrent and create deep bathing holes. I fought against the current to follow the girls, my muscles working hard to get a few yards and then had the delight of being swept downstream till I met another log and made wild yells to make Kuti and Margarita laugh. The three Ts joined us, Terra, Trisha and Tamala, the American students. We were swimming in the women's pool, the next one downstream and a little out of sight, was the men's and all this part of the river was reserved for Enrique's family and Enrique's visitors.

The three Ts were buxom and immaculate with Gone with the Wind accents. They wanted to play in the river with the children but were nervous about snakes and wild animals. But they forgot their fears quickly enough and sank into a watery bliss leaving all thought of crisps and fridge cold fizzy drinks on the bank with their clothes. We swam upstream like so many otters.

The American professors and Carlos, the minivan driver, sat at the table in Enrique's house talking. Enrique who I'd met in the garden and who had enlightened me on the purgative virtues of epazote. This large main room was furnished by a table, some homemade benches and log stools set on an earth floor. Various woven baskets and a torn hammock hung on a wall made of upright sticks. A large fridge whirred away and in it cold drinks glistened through the glass door. I limited myself to three a day. The heat gave me a craving for carbonated sweetness, plain water seemed to convert straight into sweat. Daughters and grandchildren passed through to the kitchen on one side and the private rooms on the other.

Kuti and Margarita brought out paper and pencils and begged me to test them with sums. This was manageable, basic primary school multiplication, although it took a while for us to untangle adding up from times. We went to sit on a bench outside the open door, the overhanging roof shading us. Beyond this porch with its tubs of bizzy lizzy, heaps of maize cobs dried, the sun bleaching the leaves and stalks.

As staff, Elisa, me and Carlos the driver were given the cabaña by the side of the main house. This was the storeroom Elisa promised for us. Four beds, each with a ripped or not so ripped mosquito net squeezed in among mystery boxes and sacks of fish food for another of the many cooperative enterprises supported by the government to help Lacanha survive.

The Americans unpacked their sun cream, stomach medicine and mosquito repellent in cabañas one up in comfort from ours, they had plank wood walls and netted windows that made airy rooms, and they were near the toilets with an oil drum filled with water to sluice the modern toilet bowl. The two really classy cabañas further along looked new, and had indoor toilets, hot water and a verandah. These belonged to a university. Any guest academics here could look out into the rainforest through their big mosquito proof glass windows.

I helped Elisa sort out food for supper; pasta and tins of tomatoes for a sauce, nothing that could worry the students about hygiene or health.

'Any vegetables, Enrique?'

'No rain, no vegetables.' Enrique replied. 'And the chilera bird has taken all the chillies. You're the gardener, why don't you bring me vegetables?'

'I did, I brought spinach, Enrique, but I thought you would have something here as well.'

'I'm waiting and always waiting for the rains,' for a moment he sounded serious. It was all upside down, the rains. Rainstorm in the mountains, when I arrived more than a month ago now, well before the rainy season and here, not even a spring rain.

'When it rains, then I can plant a new crop and next time you come I will feed you with squash, maize, beans, everything and burn your tongue with chillies,' and he laughed.

Enrique moved between Maya and Spanish, a conversation with visitors and family all mixed together. His five daughters were all there, four with their own children also mainly daughters. Elisa and I went into the kitchen and set a big pot of water on the metal grill and pushed long logs into the flames, the fire place a square wooden table filled with a bed of earth at waist height. The fire was laid on this and the grill set on the three hearthstones.

Washed dishes were stacked in a basket then left perched on a stool, daughters and children wandered through from main room to kitchen and out of the side door, Enrique's wife poked the logs about, and his eldest daughter put the dough through the grinder several times over until it was fine and soft, ready to go into the tortilla press.

Everything was the exact opposite of a practical, sensible kitchen. Lots of cooks and helpers and no one person doing one thing. Haphazard and homely, always someone to talk to, no one worried about what time it was or who hadn't done what. I took the spinach and accompanied by Kuti and Margarita, rinsed it outside the kitchen door in a bowl. This was spinach carried for seven hours from Na Bolom's garden to Lacanha in the rainforest.

Elisa's cooking method was simple, we pushed bunches of spaghetti pasta into the boiling water and when cooked and the water boiled down, she added tins of tomatoes and salt.

'What about garlic?' I asked,

'No, they don't like garlic,'

'Shall I add the spinach?'

'No, they're worried about eating vegetables.'

Elisa and I ate the spinach. The spaghetti and tomatoes were just what the students wanted, plus extra ketchup. Dinner at the long table was perfect, the food plentiful and filling, the fridge drinks cold, conversation wide ranging in Spanish, English and Maya. Enrique sat and ate with us. The rest of the family joined in at unpredictable moments, looking at us or sitting down or eating an extra bowl dished up by Elisa.

One daughter lay in the torn hammock with her year old son at the breast. He fell asleep and she left him slung in the net folds. Kuti and Margarita swung him from side to side and made me anxious at their vigour. Enrique told a tiger story and I hoped that would distract me from the perils nearby. Was he frightened I wanted to know? Enrique laughed, 'Yes, I was frightened, but he went away.'

I heard other tiger stories over the visits to the selva, to Lacanha and to Naha, a smaller and more remote community. I longed to see a forest creature, any one of the four big cats would do, a tigre as they called the jaguar, or a snake, a wild pig, even a tepescuintle or deer and although I did see animals and birds, most were too well aware of a human presence and hid. Animals have more reason to be afraid than we have. Their idea of ecological co existence is to watch out for us.

Later that night I saw Enrique take a rifle and a torch from a beam overhead. He smiled at me and said, 'I've left my watch on a log in the milpa,' and shaking the rifle teased, 'I might meet something I want to eat, or that might want to eat me.'

But before it was dark Elisa and I set off along the white road to see her friends, and Kuti and Margarita ran after us. The shrilling insects and bird calls were loud, and a cloud of sulphur yellow butterflies danced around the children. This 'road' was white like the ancient 'sac bec' the limestone block roads that ran between the temples and palaces of the stone cities. Our road was basic and rough, sufficient for the few vans and cars, and we walked without seeing anyone else.

I followed Elisa wherever she went, caught up in her enthusiasm for the network of friends and families she knew as Na Bolom's health worker. We were going to see the couple at the local shop. It was hard to believe in a shop when the forest towered up behind wooden houses dotted about in their own separate clearings.

It didn't look like a shop, just another house set back from the road in the middle of another milpa waiting to be planted, except that a hatch window was open. and we went up to see who was at home. A plump woman with a long plait appeared against a shelf with a few tins and sweet jars. Margarita and Kuti chose 5 pesos worth of sweets each and hung around for a bit as Elisa and the woman talked, and then ran back home.

Invited into the house through a side door, we sat in white plastic chairs and drank more cans of cold lemonade and watched television with Nuk and her husband, Kin. Kin lay in his hammock, one arm behind his head following the daily telenovela, family intrigues overacted in smart suits or sexy dresses. Kin, like Enrique, like all the Lacandon men, was dressed in a cool and simple white cotton tunic, his black hair left long, with wispy black straggles around chin and upper lip.

Sitting there in a spacious plank house with earth floor, the only furniture a fridge and a big television, we were united by the gripping but labyrinthine plot. When I ate out at Gato Gordo, I saw the news and ignored the football, but here in Nuk and Kin's home even a foreigner and a friend from Na Bolom wasn't enough live entertainment to distract them from Mexico's most popular plot.

Nuk leaned over to me, pointed at the short older man with moustache, 'He is the father, a very bad man,' and smiled. Lots of onscreen secretive, and usually interrupted, phone conversations explained the action, that is when I could catch the words. A cancelled wedding provided plenty of arguments, door slamming, and motives only we the viewers understood. And every time a woman appeared, weeping, pouting, eyes widening in astonishment at new revelations, we laughed ourselves silly.

Elisa was quite capable of talking and watching, and Nuk was soon drawn into conversation, curious that I had come here to the

Lacandon when I had a family in my own country. We managed to congratulate each other on our shared status as grandmothers, chich from my few words of Maya, and soon I was being asked how long since I stopped having periods and how many grandchildren I had, a three way conversation with Elisa translating when necessary.

A small movement at the window. Another customer. I turned to see a man with swollen half closed eyes, his long hair dull. He stood there, uninterested in friends and townie visitors. Nuk got up, the keeper of necessities, in a scene enacted in every rural place in the world, the shopfront window in someone's front room or back door. We couldn't hear the few words, but still turned towards them as if we were the residents staring at a stranger, wanting to know their business.

Elisa leant over and said, in English, 'That's the man that nearly got Fabi sacked.'

At the counter, the man pointed to a tin on the narrow, thinly stocked shelf. Nuk handed it over, no money clinked into the glass jar. Perhaps she has a little book, or its equivalent, with his name and the goods, like the front room shop in Sussex. There was an imaginary privacy when the postmaster's wife popped out as the door bell jangled, cigarette in hand, she in peach tights and no skirt, mistakenly believing herself invisible below the waist high counter. Our children, somehow unnoticed by us, the parents, ordered forbidden goods, sweets then cigarettes, on our credit. Here there was only one room, spacious and nothing unseen.

Nuk returned to us, and her customer's white shape carrying one small tin, disappeared into the dusk and the trees.

'Alcoholic,' she said. 'He works hard but then drinks all the money. His wife left, and he has no one to make his food.' A succinct biography. Wives and food, so close a link that a Mayan widower often has the new wife lined up as he buries the first. Nuk handed us a sweet each, and before we could get involved in the intrigues onscreen, I asked Elisa, 'You mean the man who went to the trustees? The other week? The man who complained that Na Bolom gave the Lacandon visitors the worst rooms and no food.'

'That's him. I was so worried about Fabi, you saw the trustees in that little room and the door closed. Even I was not allowed in with her. Of course, all that was stupid, the Lacandon families always have those rooms since Trudy and you know they can have breakfast and supper with everyone else.'

'It must be more than that, surely. It's a big deal to demand the director is sacked.'

'He is an angry man, and drinks and makes trouble.'

Fabiola had looked paler even than usual and Elisa grave and preoccupied. Na Bolom simmered with anxiety. Cecilia was in her element, guardian of information, cornering whoever she could to whisper in a corridor or the library garden. Grateful I had a straight-forward position, I heard the gossip or the real facts in instalments from anyone who just had to unburden herself, sometimes himself, to the foreign gardener.

'Fabi is like a friend,' Elisa continued, 'so I can't say everything. But it's true, it is much more than that.'

One rumour was that someone had died in one of those garden rooms, and a delay around responding to this was the real source of the fraught meetings. Serious looking men in suits appeared smoking cigarillos, joined by Doña Bety with a pinched face, trustees I'd only seen at exhibition openings or announcing a big donation to staff gathered in the library. They were responsible for Na Bolom and it's reputation. At last the air of a hospital waiting room lifted, Fabiola's reputation cleared and her status confirmed. Elisa returned to her cheerful, carefree self but Doña Bety shook her head at me and said, 'Does she ever go to the forest? Does she care about the people? Trudy would turn in her grave.'

In the forest shop, Elisa said, 'You know, it's not so easy being the health worker,' and began a more immediately pressing enquiry into her dream,

'What does it mean, Kin, a snake casting its skin?'

Kin wouldn't rouse himself, uninterested in being a sage at that moment and carried on watching the secrets and lies of Mexican city dwellers.

The small Lacandon community is so essential to demonstrating the government's commitment to protecting the rainforest that statements by one person are taken very seriously and investigated immediately. State and regional money is channeled into supporting the preservation of this forest and the longest established residents, the Lacandon Maya are essential to this.

If their life in the forest is viable their presence prevents, as far as this is possible, landless campesinos creating new villages and farms. Government subsidies ensure the allegiance of the Lacandon Maya. Some of these illegal settlers are zapatistas, members of EZLN, the Zapatista Army of National Liberation, founded and based in the forests of Chiapas. On our way into the Montes Azules, militant slogans and murals on fences surrounded certain villages, murals of men, women and children faces hidden by kerchiefs like cowboy bandits on dusty plains.

If the children grow up and remain here in Lacanha and in the other related communities of Naha and Metza Bok, then they ensure a small but fierce local defence against guerilla activity. The Lacandon Maya also keep a kind of balance between much bigger and more obviously powerful interests. There are the big commercial groups, logging, prospecting for oil, tourism development, pharmaceutical research and even the international and national environmental groups, each of which has its own agenda.

The Lacanha I saw was an arrangement of family cabins, each obscured from the others by the trees and undergrowth, each stick and palm thatch construction blending into the undefined area of river and forest which is an extended home. There were perhaps two hundred people. A tiny group of humans among a forest that holds so much importance.

Grants and funds from several charitable and government organisations go to small agricultural and craft cooperatives to support sustainable economic development. If young people like Enrique's fourteen year old son, Kayum, leave to work in the town, and they do, then there's no one to make invaders, desperate for a patch of land, think twice before they clear trees and set up home.

The Lacandon Maya have long had a formidable reputation among their Tzeltal and Tzotzil neighbours in the hills. The 'longhairs' prowess with bows and arrows and ability to survive among the wild creatures in the forest endowed them with a supernatural advantage in the past and that reputation still lingered. For the moment, I thought it kind of Nuk to give the sad man a tin and accept that he couldn't pay. I guessed it wasn't the first time.

On the way back to Enrique's we passed a courting couple, standing close in among moonlit shadows. Privacy is often somewhere out of doors for rural teenagers everywhere and here it was just a few yards along the path. In the dusk we nearly walked into them. The girl must be from Enrique's family, still in her home area as long as it's within a certain distance down the road or on particular forest paths or the section of the river where we swam on our first day.

Next evening after supper but well before dark, Carlos took us, just me and Elisa, to the highway and dropped us a couple of kilometres along and again we walked into the forest where every so often a house appeared among the trees. Atanasio's home was hard to find, I had to trust Elisa to get us there or return us to Carlos. An albino man came towards us unsurprised by our presence and immediately took up some old conversation he must have had months before. He did direct us though, pointing into the darkening trees. 'Over there, it's not far.'

Eventually we scrambled through a gap in some shrubs and saw the man Elisa looked for, lying in a hammock under a palm shelter. Elisa needed to see him, to check how he was getting on with new medication for diabetes. He indicated logs for us to sit on, and rested his hand on a stick, a big pot of water boiled on a fire. Sounds came from a plank house a few feet away, Elisa looked confused. She pointed to it.

'Is that your house?' she asked.

'No, that's Manuel Castellano's.'

'So, where is yours?' Elisa continued.

'Here. This is my house.' he said, smiling slightly with lowered eyes.

I saw her for the first time unable to find words, shocked. One hammock, a few shelves to keep food off the ground, a fire and a rotting palm thatch roof. No protection from seasonal rain and heat, or the chill damp at night, and nothing of the atmosphere of Kin and Nuk's or Enrique's that said home rather than a shelter. The trees were close by, big mature trees, as if this was once just a storeplace.

A boy came out of the shadows and stood on the edge of the eight square feet of earth where the basics of living were gathered. He was about nine years old, shy and handsome, wearing a white tunic, his feet bare. Elisa called him to her but he stayed on the edge of the firelight until she held out a large packet of sweets and he turned to his father. Then Atanasio nodded to him to accept Elisa's present. The boy looked pleased and stood there for a few minutes before moving away, and I heard the silver paper tearing.

Elisa started to talk earnestly to Atanasio, asking him about the fungus on his leg, and he pulled up the tunic to show her. It looked pitiful, a damp brown crust right along the shin bone. And when she told him how important it was to take the medicine, he got up and took a bottle of pills from the shelves to show her dutifully that he was taking his medicine. All these movements needed minimal effort as everything was so near at hand, everything Atanasio did or said was quiet and with a reserved smile. He listened to Elisa, spoke little himself, leaning back in his string hammock, occasionally putting an arm out to move the long logs further under the pot of water.

Elisa's plainness was admirable, 'Does he go to school? No? He must go, you know that. And he will love it, he needs to be like the other children.'

Atanasio nodded but didn't answer. I wondered if the boy was listening from the dark beyond the fire, wondered how much Spanish he understood.

'He needs to learn, he's an intelligent boy. You can see that.'

But Atanasio wasn't going to explain how he might need his son to help him in those daily survival tasks, bringing wood and water, collecting fruits.

Elisa was 27, a city girl but without artifice at important moments, brave and compassionate. People liked Elisa. It was rare for her to be unable to joke and chat, to create a comfortable atmosphere and instead she asked Atanasio about his living, making baskets. He was the last person in Lacanha who made them and then at her suggestion he moved from the hammock, as passive there as a baby in a sling, to take a couple of round baskets from a roof beam.

'Look how perfect they are, wouldn't you love to take one home?' she encouraged. The mood between a sick unhappy man and us visiting townies lifted. The baskets were pale fine split cane and I chose the large one. It had a lovely shape, round like a nest, and tapered inwards at the top.

'How much?' I asked. Atanasio, revived but not yet so enthusiastic as us, said 30 pesos. Elisa bounced into her old self, 'Not enough!' she said, glad to be on top of things again and make us laugh. She bargained him up to 50 pesos while I listened and watched and agreed. Atanasio managing to laugh drew his son nearer, smiling, his bag of sweets held close. Atanasio accepted my money, tucking the notes into a tin.

'Keep this one for me,' Elisa ordered, examining a basket in progress, 'and I want a lid as well. So, I will be back, Atanasio.' We left through the gap in the hedge and avoided the pool of mud that looked too much like overflow from a latrine.

CHAPTER 5

Yaxchilan

It was the trip to Yaxchilan. The three Ts, the boys, the college professors settled in to the minibus. The three Ts sat together, unblemished in crease free shorts, not one mosquito bite to be seen on smooth plump legs, they carried bottles of water and sun block. These girls arrived in San Cristobal keen on 'cultural studies' but dismayed by foreign food and yet they set out on every expedition in spite of expected danger and a terror of wild creatures. I who was keen on these dangers and looked for them, had been dismissive of the all American girls, scornful of their college course.

'We'll see crocodiles!' I said as I passed to my seat.

'Really!' they said with a frisson of alarm. But they never refused an experience. I was getting fond of them. All the gringos seated for optimum breeze and views, Elisa and I took our places with Enrique, his wife and son, Kayum, granddaughters Kuti and Margarita plus several other children.

Frans and Trudy Blom's photographs show the Lacandon before the road, before minivans. Their little expeditionary group spent weeks enclosed by trees, travelling with mules and enough baggage for the long journey on forest trails, they smiled at the camera as they washed in a tin bowl or unpacked in the camp. Later on I hung my own baggage from the roof struts of their old permanent camp at Naha and saw the night tme torrents of rain from my hammock.

Unlike the Bloms half a century ago, our van drove fast and alone on a good road, good due to military level maintenance. Once past the ubiquitous army check point at the New Palestine cross roads, the only traffic we saw was a black howler monkey, the size, and for a moment, the appearance of a large dog. It bounded along the gully edge before disappearing into the undergrowth. Carlos, our demon driver, put on the same old CD and his foot on the accelerator to arrive at the boarding point for our trip down the great Usumacinta river.

Kingfisher and herons, cormorants, if not the exact birds I knew in England, the same idea in grey, yellow, green, white and black. They perched on dead branches rising from the water. Kuti and Margarita pointed out spider monkeys in the trees that came down to the bank on either side. Identical landscapes to look at and once divided into the separate dominions of Mayan rulers, now it was Guatemala and Chiapas that faced each other across the Usumacinta.

An hour under the canopy of an open motor launch and the landscape remained thick and green all along, a landscape where people might well not have been invented. Enrique's grandchildren drifted off to sleep and the adults dozed under the hypnotic, humming green. Yax is the colour associated with the navel of the world, the mid point of the four directions, the entry to the spiritual world. Yax is the continuum of blue to green, the colour of water, sky, leaves and plants.

Yaxchilan, translates as 'place of the split sky', the name based on the solar alignment of the city. From one of the tall buildings an observer at the summer solstice sees the sun rise in the cleft between two mountains. One of the great Mayan temple sites from the Classic period – around 600 to 900 AD – Yaxchilan sits enclosed by jungle. The city looks out across the river into the thick forest of Guatemala. Steps lead up to a flat concourse where the stelas and stucco panels record the blood letting, vision inducing rituals with Lord Shield Jaguar and his son Bird Jaguar. The Jaguar dynasty was the most powerful and militarily successful rule of the time.

Yaxchilan made alliances with Tikal in Guatemala and Palenque, the latter now the two most splendid and successful attractions on the Mayan circuit. But Yaxchilan can only be reached by river, an archaeological treasure in deep jungle, and few visitors get there. I was selfishly glad it remained remote, took pleasure in the contrast between the limestone blocks of what was once a populous city state with temples and palaces and the steadily exuberant forest growth. In spite of the human obsession to raise monuments to the astounding knowledge and bloody triumphs of the human race, here in the Selva Lacandona the forest had closed in. It made Yaxchilan into a place of calm beauty, of Ozymandian thoughtfulness.

We walked up the bank, silenced, trespassing among the remains of ancestors, the sounds were the deep roar of howler monkeys and the warning complaints of birds in the high canopy surrounding the ruins. The only inhabitants, colonies of bats that fluttered around us as we walked through the dark damp passages that were an entry and exit.

Two little grey spider monkeys, their white tummies showing, swung across the branches. Three bright billed toucans shot across the clearing. It was impossible to lose Enrique and the students, we few were dotted about the plaza and the steps of temples. The only other visitors were an archaeologist and his two companions, I listened in as he explained the ritual blood letting and pointed out the carved detail of a woman kneeling with a basin to catch the blood from her king's penis.

'You see he is using an instrument to perforate his penis. All the soft tissue parts of the body are pierced to offer blood, the penis, the ear lobes, the tongue, to make a symbolic sacrifice. The nobler the supplicant, the greater value their blood as an offering. Royal prisoners were immensely valuable as sacrifices.'

The archaeologist's companions and I stood riveted. The archaeologist continued, 'In return for pain and blood, he is granted visions. In another stela his wife assists him by drawing a string laced with thorns through his tongue.' The ornate relief carvings clarified as he spoke.

There's only so many archaeological information labels I can read, even on such unusual wifely duties. I sat on a mound and breathed in the atmosphere allowing myself to notice what was in front of my eyes instead of cluttering my mind with thinking too much about the past. I held the heavy Russian binoculars borrowed from my birdwatching friend in England. They were so obtrusive I'd never taken them out anywhere before. I raised them ready, looking.

Lizards posed facing up or down the trunk of the tree in front of me, a brown bird moved systematically up a branch picking insects out from under the bark, a bird beautiful with subtle stripes and spots in many variations of chestnut brown and grey black. I noted all these down to look up later against one of Cecilia's reference books with detailed illustrations of birds, mammals and reptiles.

After a while, I saw a bird, the size of a pheasant, resting on a branch as comfortable and relaxed as I was. It sat opposite looking down on me; a glossy black head with a modest round crest, a yellow breast rich as egg yolk and I recognised the long tail smartly barred with grey. Recognised it from browsing books looking for pictures of the resplendent quetzal. This bird was a trogon of some sort, belonging to the same family as the resplendent quetzal, whose metre long tail feathers crowned Lord Bird Jaguar's braided hair on the carvings around me.

The splendid costumes of the Mayan lords reminded them, and their subjects, of their ritual significance. The jaguar, whose skins made royal robes, symbolized contact with the gods and the undulating quetzal feathers the movement of day to night, creation to destruction. Before I arrived in Chiapas I read whatever I could about this mythic bird, emerald green with a crimson red breast, and decided if I could return home having seen a glimpse of one iridescent feather I would be supremely fulfilled. There were many obstructions to this quest and

I discovered that the only time to see the resplendent quetzal is in the Spring mating season up in the remote cloud forest of El Triunfo. It was already early summer and past the season when the male quetzal needed to delight the female.

Like other creatures that hold a symbolic and ecologically charged power the quetzal needs a large and undisturbed area. An area which has plenty of its main food, the wild avocado. Knowing this rare and beautiful bird ate green fruit, somehow added to my fascination. Biospheres and reserves exist but as highways penetrate, other things follow and creatures retreat along with the wilderness.

I was in Yaxchilan and looking at a relative of the quetzal and that was some satisfaction. We stayed here for half an hour or so, the trogon and I, staring at each other companionably. As a bird it reminded me more of a chicken than anything, that comfortable settledness of its posture, the matronly stare and the occasional way it looked about. Except that it was a beautiful creature.

Time to go, I caught up with the group and we posed for a photo by the river. I picked up a pebble and climbed into the lancha.

On the way back Enrique told us he had been to Yaxchilan many times as a younger man. Those discussions in the library at Na Bolom or at the supper table about whether the Lacandon still practised their religion, or took part in the old ceremonies came back to me. I listened as Enrique spoke about Yaxchilan as the place the men went to burn copal incense and drink balché to honour the gods. When Trudy began her enduring friendship with the Lacandon, this was certainly a living practice led by Chan Kin Viejo, the last respected spiritual and community leader.

In the last decades of the 20th century many of the Lacandon converted to evangelical protestantism but it wasn't clear what remained, or not, of earlier ways of worship. Just as families used both the traditional names like Chan Kin, little sun, and Christian names, Enrique or Atanasio, so old and new ways merged and blurred.

The lancha took us back to have lunch at the restaurant overlooking the river, another somnolent, humid hour along the Usumacinta, waving to the occasional man on the Guatemalan bank.

Elisa and the college professors had packed every kind of experience into the trip for their students. Carlos took us to whatever and wherever it was. The engine driving the air conditioning which made a background to the three Ts' conversations on state of the moment stomachs. Every so often, Gordon or Greg, knowledgeable but low key professors, came up with a mini lecture and Elisa and I talked quietly, the subject of our conversations – the whereabouts of Elisa's love, Cesar – much too intense and important to be overheard by others.

'So is Cesar still in the forest, the same place?'

'Oh Bernardina, it is so hard for me, I know why Cesar needs to go and live in the selva with the Maya. Why he has to do this alone?'

I'd seen it before, this exclusion from the important moments. Was he afraid of being inept in front of his girl friend, not looking cool. Town boy humiliated by hard work, stinging insects and hole in the ground toilets. I could be wrong.

'You come here to Chiapas alone,' Elisa carried on, 'You want to know us, know Mexico. You can understand Cesar too.'

Yes, that was true, and that was why I was reserved towards the professors and their tour, I wouldn't 'know' Mexico unless I kept my aloneness. This was not something I could, or wanted to keep up while river swimming in jungle and eating together at Enrique's. I resisted gravitating towards English speakers or Europeans because at the very least, I would never learn Spanish, never learn it through thinking differently, or finding new ways of saying things. Maybe I did understand Cesar, like Elisa said.

'So is he near here?' I asked. 'near Lacanha ? Will you see him?'

'He isn't here in the Lacandon. You mustn't tell, but he is in a

EZLN community, the Lacanha community don't like the EZLN. I will go too, but another EZLN community, go on my own.'

I was confused. Community was a loose arrangement of settlements and villages, like a rural parish except that the majority of the inhabitants would be a distinct branch of the Maya, Tzeltal or Tzotzil or Lacandon. I had an image of Cesar in this kind of community with the white tunic men and the stories about Kisin, the dark lord, who shakes the earth when he's angry. I saw Cesar learning to live alongside the forest plants, getting along with other young men like Enrique's son in law who talked about the wild local scandals, coping with the man with the burnt hand who threatened his lover with a machete but struck an electrical cable.

I had to think again, and learn to see Cesar among armed and masked men. We've passed signs at the entrance to rebel villages with these words, 'communidad autonomo - independiente - rebelde' and painted in black, a man in a balaclava, gun propped against a shoulder. It felt strange and uncomfortable that someone I knew was willing to use a gun; the old socialist struggles of the 20th century for land and liberty were far away in time and in a way of thinking. Death and revolution in Mexico, Cuba, Nicaragua had seemed noble, worthwhile, in the 1960s.

Unlike the campesinos, no one threatened my plot of land, no one denied me education, I didn't travel miles for a doctor or lose a day's earnings to do so. I supported big causes outside my family sized world, I saw that other reality only in selected images. But I was affected at a distance. It was for me to agree to or resist the larger world I lived in. I needed to choose what kind of world I supported, and part of my choice was knowing the natural world, planting new woods at home in Suffolk, staying in the Chiapas rainforest and seeing for myself the burning trunks in newly cleared land. My choice was eating fresh food grown without pesticides. I saw campesinos walking along the roads the plastic tanks on their backs ready to poison plants, and slowly the sprayer. I saw the rural tiendas plastered with posters; Rival, Paraquat.

My choice also included thinking about the frightening parts of resistance here in Chiapas, the guns and who used them. Cesar? Nowhere was free from disturbing choices. The Lacandon Maya and their forest home, promoted as a place of interdependent harmony was not any simpler, or more peaceful, than any other community.

The young mothers came to visit on our last day at Lacanha, each with a baby in a cloth sling tied in a big knot on one shoulder for easy transfer from back to breast. They clustered outside Enrique's house talking to Elisa, or aided by Carlos, they packed their forest goods, bark string bags, seed bracelets, wooden forks and spoons, in a box to be sold in Na Bolom's shop. The three Ts, large and pale under their hats and sun cream, looked at the babies and tried to make them smile.

'Where can I find Kayum Maax and Chanakin?' I asked.

'Come with us, we'll show you. Ko'ox!' they called to their friends, 'Let's go.' And we walked down towards the little airstrip and a first aid hut, rather worryingly placed near to it, I thought, mothers and babies at shoulder height around me.

'Go along that path past the bamboo, then further on you will see Kayum Maax' house.'

And they left me, disappearing one by one into the forest to follow their own paths. I walked between canes higher than my head, the dry leaves rubbing and rustling as my passing disturbed the heavy, damp air. Late morning, birds and even insect sounds stopped, the calls of people and children became muted and then excluded by the thick growth behind me. I slowed down, aware of my aloneness. How rare. And how rarely I missed my loved and needed times of solitude, But now I savoured it, feeling every step, every movement among this midday stillness, my sight sharpened to every unknown tree and vine.

Trees and undergrowth, clearer now not pressing upon me from either side but no glimpse of a roof. Turning round to make sure I knew my way back, I noted where the gap in the cane tangle began. Further on still, a tin roof and I called out, 'Kayum? Chanakin?' and a man came out, a strong, big chested man, and a young girl. He stood smiling but looking far away, 'I'm looking for Kayum Maax.'

'Not here, further.' And then he wanted to know who I was as if I was a welcome distraction. 'I cannot see you,' and he pointed to his eyes, which I saw were unfocused, inexpressive, 'but I like to talk. It's not many people who come by.'

I was too fixated on finding my way to have anything to say to this oblique invitation.

'Go with my daughter, perhaps I will meet you at Na Bolom. I'll ask for you.'

The girl walked me to a point where I heard voices and saw people under an open thatch roof, and Chanakin in her red flowered shift rolling tortilla dough on a flat open basket. She laughed when she saw me, and Kayum looked round. He didn't look so happy.

'So now you come to see us. The last day,' he said, but he pulled up a low wooden chair for me. Chanakin carried on rolling and patting and piling up tortillas and smiling. 'Water,' she said, 'get her some water.'

At least I imagined I heard those words as Kayum brought me a glass. Spanish and English and Maya criss crossed life at Na Bolom and I assumed I knew exactly what was being said. That is I understood if I didn't stop to think. We sat and talked in the open to the air room, really a roof for shade and a waist high stick wall. Kayum impressed on me how he had visitors too, 'From the capital, they come to stay here, stay with me, Trudy would want that. Na Bolom doesn't look after everyone in the selva, you know, even though I was the one who lived there. You know my room?'

'Is it the room in the little courtyard? That's Marie's office now?'

But his thoughts had run on. 'So much money, you know they have so much but does it come here?'

'I heard it used to be like a big family at Na Bolom, when Trudy was alive.' I said helpfully, before I remembered that both of Trudy's protegées, Doña Bety and Kayum had displeased her, Doña Bety by getting married and Kayum by refusing education.

'How would I know?' he said. 'My parents died and I have no children.'

Chanakin looked worried as she watched his face, interpreting the mood sounds of our Spanish words. 'Come on, I will walk you to the path. They will leave you in the forest if they know you've come to visit Kayum Maax!'

As I walked back alone again with time to think about the forest and the people who lived here, the only real knowledge I'd gained was that no one would regard forest life for Enrique, Atanasio or Kayum, each so different in situation and personality, as one of simplicity or harmony. No one would doubt that the 'longhairs' were still a challenge for more settled neighbours.

Carlos turned off the highway and down towards the entrance to Agua Azul. Still in the hot lands, this was our last stop before climbing towards other mountains and home to Na Bolom. The multi layered waterfalls of Agua Azul were a huge, powerful natural force pounding down through forested mountains and a summer picnic spot for Mexicans on holiday.

Elisa paid the entrance fee and a few minutes later had a shouting match over a second entrance demand. 'Oh, but this is for the locals,' the young man insisted, and again that phrase, 'for the community,' but he gave up soon enough unable to cope with Elisa's fury. I pictured council tenants charging for entry into a nearby beauty spot, the bleak

Downs Estate charging to enter Hackney Marshes or walk by the River Lea. Then it was the turn of women and children selling fruit, mangoes and peaches and melons. They lined the road holding the luscious juiciness out to us. But we could see the water and heard the tumbling greeny blue falls, down from one pool to another, and couldn't wait to throw ourselves in.

The sound became normal as we changed on the grass and jumped in, swimming against the steady drag of the river to sit on the low ridge of the last fall before the river flowed away. The pools were deep and clear, a pause but with a strong current, and it took a while to feel confident that I wouldn't be whirled away downstream in a second. Held against the lip of the pool, we floated staring up at the figures as they stepped out onto the high ledge opposite. Behind them a series of wide cascades threw up white plumes in each pool. The figures stood there looking down and occasionally one leapt out and disappeared under the whirling depths.

There are moments when I'm grateful I have no desire to do that thing I am watching. I never go up on stage when volunteers are called for. I never sing in the pub session. But I watched the three Ts, then the professors, the professor's son, his wife and finally tall thin George still in his headscarf. However long they stood, one by one they leapt, more or less gracefully. I couldn't be the only one to turn away. I made my way, just to look, and met George on his way back. 'It's fine. Worth it. I felt good that I did jump.'

Touched by this kind and gentle teenager, I felt if he could do it... and slid one foot after another foot along the shallow water of the parapet anxious about walking these rock pools and tripping or slipping and falling off before I got to the main jump off point. A hundred foot walk of nerves until I stood mid point.

There was no expected churn of adrenalin, just a dull resignation. I shuffled as far to the edge as I could and remain upright, looked out at the smooth roll of water like liquid blue glass, the hot sky and the laughing people holding to a rope stretched across the river below me. I had to push through the air to beyond where the water plummeted. I ordered my legs which moved in numb obedience, run, run, and leapt as far out as I could. Tumbled and rolled far down, then squeezed and popped out, I rose mouth open like an astonished fish.

CHAPTER 6

One Heart

'A well weeded plant is of one heart and industrious'

FROM THE TZOTZIL

People stopped to talk as I worked in the garden. I provided the industrious part and the conversation of one heart arose. There's something about being practical and purposeful that attracts. This morning an American photographer, here to take photographs of Mexican writers, lingered with his friend, Peter, a friend who seemed a bit at a loose end, just travelling as company.

Peter returned later to sit on the pedestal ledge of Diego Rivera's statue and confided how aimless he feels moving every few days, watching one face after another being recorded. I understood because I needed to be here, in one place and see the results of my actions, even if I had do the same thing again every few days. But I listened and responded to him while digging and the pile of weeds grew.

I was getting to be a mild version of an agony aunt. Always there so she, or he, asked what I was doing and then moved on to other subjects; usually what they were doing and how they felt about it, helped by the fact that my ear turned towards them and my face turned away. One day several men turned up at once while I hoed the beetroot; Peter and the photographer joined Karl, tall and fit who was telling me about the cycle trip to Tenejapa to which I had reluctantly said no.

Invitations were a reminder of the commitment I made to working here, working every week day, all day. A commitment to honour not only my arrangement with Na Bolom, my host, but also the decision I made on my last birthday to step outside my safe zone and reach out for something new, and work at it. Of course, there was a secondary thought to my refusal. Cycling to Tenejapa? How were my leg muscles? I wanted Peter to find a passion that would make him be unable to accept invitations to go along with someone else's.

Manvel glanced over. He was amused by the male fan club although it didn't happen often enough to be embarrassing. I was flattered, and energised. Manvel preferred to work alone, and I had given up trying to be his assistant. I'd learnt to think for myself in this garden but I liked these unexpected companions. Stopping to talk they were responsive to the garden too, in their different ways.

Young women were more likely to pause here, relax and get a bit of surrogate mothering. Helen, a Dutch girl, clever and independent, returned one day on her way through from the Yucatan beach to Oaxaca and spent the day helping me. It pleased her like it pleased me to do something that had a visible satisfaction.

We worked together to clear the weeds and leaves from a patch between the office and the archive. The roses were neatly deadheaded, the geraniums uncovered under the green foliage of elephant ear plants and the jasmine roots freed from a mass grave of paper scraps and cigarette butts. Then I walked her down Calle Adelina Flores to the main plaza where the band played that soft focus latin swing that reminded me of my childhood, and the Edmundo Ros band on the BBC. We hugged goodbye, a brief friendship, and she turned down to the bus station; blonde with knapsack.

There were other garden conversations that introduced me to new aspects of Chiapas. Koh Maria and Koh Paniagua, the widows of

Chan Kin Viejo, Trudy Blom's great friend, were rather like the royal family of the rainforest Maya. All members of the family were accorded respect because of their relative. And although Chan Kin Viejo died a few years ago reputably aged 101, he left two children still in the family home. Polygamy, still practised in his pre evangelist lifetime, ensured as many children as possible. The youngest, Daniel Chan Kin, was nine years old, and he had the same distinctive pouting lower lip as I saw in the many photographs of his venerable father. The widows and children came to stay in the rooms reserved for any visitor from the Lacandon.

Chan Kin Viejo's family had a special feeling about them, the modest and private demeanour of people from a small rural place. They lived in Naha, the most remote and traditional community of about 130 individuals where wives still wore the old style long flowered skirts and short white tunics. Each of Chan Kin Viejo's wives, had a plait decorated at the end with toucan and eagle feathers, emblems of the married woman. Although I met many women who made a good balancing act between forest life and town, Koh Maria and Koh Paniagua were content to be who they are.

So I felt disturbed when I witnessed a Mexico City couple buying necklaces from the elder wife. The woman selected a couple of strings of the distinctive forest seeds, one red and black, the other having a large 'deer's eye' pendant and she, the buyer, drove a hard bargain. It was like watching the three card trick I saw years ago in Charing Cross Road.

'How much are these?' she asked, 'And this one? And what about these other ones?' And she swapped them around, laying one down and picking another, ending with two beauties, repeating the prices for the simplest necklaces selected earlier. Quite a performance, the sort you would expect from a experienced market buyer. Koh Maria, with minimal Spanish and not experienced enough, was assisted by her seventeen year old daughter. 'This one is 20 pesos and the longer necklace is 25,' she told her.

'15 and 20,' said the woman and turned to her husband displaying her choice while ignoring the mother and daughter as they explained that the best price must be 20 and 25 pesos, as these were gathered seeds, colorines, and hand strung with a proper clasp. The woman merely said, 'and I'll have them both so here's 30 pesos the two.' And the couple walked away leaving Koh Maria and Chanuk overwhelmed and me furious on their behalf at such cavalier behaviour.

My own collection was accumulating; several strings with the red and black colorine seeds, a subtle necklace with small brown seeds and a few fat, flat seeds, called ibikash, brown and black with a white side stripe like a deer's eye, and another of tiny shiny seeds that might be linseed, looking temptingly delicious. I regret that I didn't know their latin or european names.

I was learning all the time, asking Manvel simple questions and getting answers I couldn't always remember, but I recorded as much as possible at the end of the day. When Doña Bety walked by on her way to and from her house over the workshop and toolshed in the opposite corner of the garden to Manvel's hut, I asked her the plant names I'd forgotten. It was a way to reach her. We were becoming accustomed to each other.

And for my break I got a herb tea from the kitchen or, if Angel was in an amenable mood, coffee, and I walked the paths mug in hand, identifying blooms and repeating under my breath, 'foquito, azucena, perrito, juanita, escovilla, tulipan.' That is, before I met Tito and acquired a whole new litany of latin and popular orchid names.

Fabiola, the director, mentioned that there was a man in town who had become an amateur expert on orchids and that he would probably be willing to give me some guidance on caring for Na Bolom's neglected collection. The mention of this man was accompanied by a smile from Fabiola, and Elisa said, 'I wonder what you'll make of Tito.' This together with the 'probably' brought up the image of a maverick, in a land where mavericks were humoured.

'Bernardine, I hear you want to see my orchids.' I saw a quizzical face with iron grey curls springing from head and chin. 'Tito.' And he held out a hand. Our first and only straightforward conversation I ever had with this gifted orchid collector. Other times the talk bounded from the behaviour of pollinating bees to a bawdy anecdote about a man who sat on a stinging caterpillar to the intricacies of making cohuetes, the firecrackers that celebrate just about everything. The firecracker was a suitable emblem for Tito, with its precision and good timing creating plenty of sound and dazzle.

By this time I knew the garden well enough to show him the orchids that were in bloom. A well established cluster clung to a tall oak and every time I walked through from garden to inner courtyard and back I saw the white curved petals cascading down the trunk at eye level.

'*Epidendrum parkinsonianum*,' said Tito, 'you see both the petals and lip are white, but here,' he continued as we moved round the other side of the oak, 'Epidendrum radioferens, has speckled purple brown petals with a green lip.'

'Lip' I echoed,

'Yes,' he smiled, 'an attractive landing place for the pollinator.'

This orchid even with several blooms along each stem, was less showy, the colours and speckles matching the tree, but under Tito's guidance, the more I looked at each species, the more I began to notice subtle beauties.

He pointed out dozens of orchids I had overlooked, clumps fallen to the ground and obscured by dead pine needles, tied to trees I rarely walked by, in pots on windowsills. I learnt that although the majority are epiphytic there are also terrestrial orchids, and some of the epiphytic orchids had been planted in soil which caused Tito to go into shock horror mode. I followed him around the garden making notes as fast as I could, trying to look at all that he pointed out at the same time as recording what needed replanting and how. I felt like the Emperor's chancellor taking down orders and information and making assurances to his majestic person that I understood perfectly.

'Oh, how could anyone do this!' he exclaimed, 'Pine needles are anathema to orchids. Oak mulch, oak mulch, that's what they love. You never see orchids growing on pines, oak, cypress, yes. Get Manvel to bring you some oak mulch from Chamula, it's all oak up there, lots of wonderful composta.'

I began to feel responsible for the well being of these orphaned orchids and I hadn't even noticed most of them or seen that they lay neglected in unsuitable conditions. So far I lacked the art of asking the resident gardeners successfully for anything more than basic requests. I had an Oliver complex, holding out my bowl tentatively, sure of refusal. Now I had a mission. I would ask Manvel for oak composta from Chamula. But I hadn't quite arrived at this new assertive sense of purpose.

'Tito, how am I going to remember all this. Where do I begin?' I said, staring at my notes and then the garden. 'I've made a list. Move orchids. Get oak mulch. But what about identify varieties? I've written some names but...'

'Come and see my garden,' he said, as if this would provide all the answers, or at least clues to my orchid challenge. 'Just a few minutes from here, give me a call first.'

Tito saw I must start with one simple task after this disturbing grand tour. And he took my notebook and pen and drew several diagrams.

'This is how I make labels,' he explained, 'Recycle your beer cans. Or coke if you prefer. They don't disintegrate in the rain and the writing doesn't wear off. As they bloom, identify and label.' He handed my book back with clearly set out conversion steps: cans to labels.

'Must leave you now. Knock loudly, I may be in the dark room and I love loud music.'

I needed to sit down. I had orchid overload. My favourite spot was a cement bench and table, one corner broken open showing the metal rods, but shaded by a fragrant arch of honeysuckle. I made a list. That was the first step. Putting an order into all the flood of information calmed me. I worked backwards:

> Beer can labels – would mine look as good as Tito's sketch
> Ask Manuel to bring a bag of oak mulch from Chamula
> Dig up coelia machrostachya and make a new bed of stones, cover with compost, must be oak, and replant leaving pseudobulbs clear
> Pots on windowsill by dining room: drill drainage holes in base, add plenty of stones and replace soil with oak mulch
> Replace orange or blue plastic twine holding orchids to trees with copper wire,
> Urgent! Move all orchids from pine trees and rehome

Tito said fruit trees were fine too; there were plenty of peach, apricot known as durazno, and plum trees, ciruelas, which threw down quantities of small round yellow fruits called hog plums. I saw hairy ginger pigs tethered by the roadside and wanted to send a picture to Marcus, my pig farmer neighbour in Suffolk. I liked the idea of plum fed pork. My list went on and on, and as I began to implement my tasks over the next days and weeks, the phrase 'Tito says' became my special call like the squeaks of the humming birds or the strange tones of the wedgetailed grackle that made me wish someone would answer the phone.

As one of the gardeners, I felt a certain satisfaction and security by then in having marked out a territory that showed, Bernardine is here; the medicine plants kept clear of pine fronds in dark earth nicely forked over, Diego Rivera's statue womanising and bibulous among a happy surge of roses, perritos and juanitas. Now I was inundated by a whole new vision of plant demands. I went to the kitchen bold enough to order a supply of empty cans.

'Why don't you come and take lunch by the library?' Cecilia called on her way back there with her camomile tea. She wore so many clothes; today she had added white stockings and a small shawl over an embroidered cardigan. It was chilly in the library, but refreshing for me sweaty from exerting myself through the hot part of the day. I followed her with my picnic; manchego cheese, a couple of red jitomates, – only green ones are called tomatoes, – and a big fat mango. Fresh picked they cost four for 5 pesos from a woman sitting on the ledge of a pavement near the market.

All my excess waist padding had melted away and every tastebud eagerly awaited the difference between salty cheese and the particular sweetness of peppery tomato and then the juiciness of mango. I licked my fingers and went to chat in Spanish and English with Cecilia.

Our daily lunch talks were mainly in Spanish as Cecilia was too self conscious to speak in my language, which suited me. She wanted to talk, it could be lonely in the library, there were plenty of visitors but they were there to do research and sat reading with laptops or notepads. So I had a Spanish lesson every lunch time. This time I asked for a book as well, 'Orquideas de Chiapas' and after a restorative gossip, sat outside on the library verandah and turned the pages of large scale illustrations hoping to see something I recognised.

As the book was in Spanish, it took a while to decode the identifying words and work out how the classification was ordered. But I could do it and loved to see the information start to reveal itself. I began to link what grew outside to the concentrated biographies of these beautiful creations. I found one of those orchid names I scribbled down the day of Tito's visit, 'Osmoglossum pulchellum, flowering period March / April, colour white, scent, day.' The syllables were as luscious as the orchid bloom.

The book became my guide and my bible, I returned to it almost daily, it reminded me which plants to raise up from their earthly beds of soil. I deciphered their needs and replaced them on head height branches to nestle in cushions of rotting leaves. It gave me predictions on what flowerings to look for in which month, it taught me the common names and the botanical, and I saw the colours, speckles, spots and contrasts of each orchid flower in large scale photographs and in botanical drawings. The Orchids of Chiapas book began to look used.

Elisa found me a room. I was excited. It would be a sign of being here, a proper resident human being, not mistaken for a gringa, which I was relieved to know is specifically someone from the United States, and regarded with a mixture of scorn and envy. Graffitti focused on George Bush, or as one masterpiece had it, 'George W.C.Bush', Tony Blair as a worthwhile hate figure hadn't yet crossed the Atlantic as far as Mexico.

'A room? Where?'

'It's a house in the Barrio Mexicanos, just the other side of Santo Domingo market. Yes? You want it?'

'Why not, I'd like to have a look. When can I go and see it?'

'If you're interested, Carolina says she will come here at 4 o'clock and meet you. She's the woman I used to live next door to.'

Mmm, I thought, she wants to check me out first. OK. Frans Blom's old room with its own bath suited me very well. I enjoyed plenty of hot water steeping muscles unused to hours of regular physical work. I liked the idea that this man, author of Tribes and Temples, who journeyed by pack horse into the rainforest to look for hidden knowledge, re read his notes here, slept and dreamt here in this room. It was my refuge. I had my garden projects, finding out about the herb plants and dye plants, falling in love with the orchids, getting to know people, but then I retreated to his room. Na Bolom looked after me, almost inadvertently.

But it was time for me to move on, explore life outside. Fabiola's gracious suggestion that I stay at Na Bolom for a while had made these first months a gentle way to acclimatise. I was ready for another view of Chiapas, and a social life that didn't depend on supper guests passing through San Cristobal. Elisa was about to leave and I would miss her lively company and our long conversations about people and politics. I felt anxious that I wouldn't manage without her.

We seemed to understand each other so well, Elisa knew exactly why I was in Chiapas, why I wanted to work here at Na Bolom. When she came to the garden it was to talk about Cesar or her constantly changing plans, with someone who understood also exactly why she wanted to do whatever it was. I could identify with her longing to follow Cesar to the Montes Azules, or go and live in the rainforest, even reconsider marriage to her first boyfriend – although I stopped there because I had already adopted Cesar as an almost son in law.

I put the hoe and wheelbarrow away in the shed changed my shoes and unhooked my bag from the peg. 'Carolina's here.' Elisa called across the garden. Carolina waited in the main courtyard where the hummingbirds came to the bougainvillea in the cool of late afternoon. I saw a tall woman with very straight brown hair, arms folded, gusting clouds of smoke from plum coloured lips like a dark Marlene Dietrich.

We sat and talked. The room available had a bed and shelves, share shower with a French couple, share kitchen with everyone. She told me the rent, the address and how to get there. It sounded a bit far but … if I was ready for new events.

Then, 'How do you feel about animals, I have a cat and a dog?'

I hesitated, 'OK... so long as it's not an alsatian.'

'No, a mongrel. And she's young and friendly.'

It was all agreed. I would go and look before supper. Walk down Calle Comitan, through the market to Calle Mexicano, second turning right and look for the blue and white house on the left.

The next day I moved in and learnt the walk to and from Na Bolom. I woke in the mornings to cigarette smoke wafting up to my

grander house with walls not railings around their courtyard. The six musicians wore suits decorated with swirls of braid, they had moustaches and I knew the song was full of love even though I couldn't pick out the words. As the sky lightened the mariachi were called into the house where they sang on faintly and I returned to bed. I willed myself into a dreamy sleep where the music was for me.

At work Cecilia told me how lucky I was to hear a serenata.

'It's a traditional way to court a sweetheart, but not heard very often nowadays,' she said, then looked at me with a mixture of distrust as if I had really been the favoured recipient, not the woman next door, and scepticism if that was true.

'Today it's Mother's Day in Mexico,' she remembered, 'it must be that. It's not unusual for a man to hire a mariachi group to serenade his mother.' And she sang, 'oh, mujeres divinas,' and said, 'That's a very popular mariachi song.'

'Oh Cecilia divina,' I responded in my hopelessly unmusical voice and I knew who she would like to make a serenata for her. Patricio, younger, good looking, was one of several anthropologists who visited Na Bolom, and Cecilia so covered up in layers and self protecting in other ways, became instantly amenable to his every wish whenever he entered the library.

But the serenata had not been for Cecilia or for me and I didn't know whether to feel disappointed that all the adoration was for Mothers' Day or impressed that Mexican men cherished their mothers so much they wanted to sing to them, sing about them. There was plenty to talk about for my next Spanish lesson with Gabriel at Instituto Jovel.

Encyclia cochleata lived up to everything
flamboyant and weird in the orchid reputation
... Its local Tzotzil name, translates as 'spook's
water receptacle'.

CHAPTER 7

Living On Air

'orchids through interaction with pollinators and symbiosis with mycorrhizae fungi, are examples of the most complex floral evolution known.'

Until arriving in Chiapas my image of an orchid was an old fashioned corsage on a ball gown or the title of a crime novel. Either way it had allure and mystery and as I learnt more about the individual orchids in Na Bolom's garden, the allure became a real fascination. The first orchid I noticed was the one with the name as beautiful as its flowers, *Osmoglossum pulchellum.* Tied to a the trunk of tree, the stem of white petals arched just above eye level.

The word, orchid, from the greek '*orchis*' meaning testicle, comes from the appearance of the pseudobulbs, the swollen base of the epiphytic orchid stem and the tubers of terrestrial ones. The similarity ends there as one plant multiplies into a mass with many pseudobulbs. Theophrastos, considered to be the father of botany and ecology, was the first to use the name in his book of natural history some time around 300 BC.

In Mexico orchids have been appreciated, and some cultivated, at least since Aztec times when *Vanilla planifolia* was used to flavour chocolatl, the fabulously delicious ritual drink of kings and nobles. In the world of orchids, Chiapas is home to half of all the species in

Mexico, approximately 600. In Na Bolom's garden I tracked down 38, and others appeared when I believed I had found them all.

For a week I watched orchid buds swell on a tree along the path to the photographic archive and the guest rooms. There were three plants on this tree and the budding one was exactly at eye level, but they seemed to take forever to reach the stage when I could glimpse a colour, a shape, possible markings. I waited and waited to make my first independent identification.

Cecilia provided guidance on reference books, opening ones that had a chapter on high altitude plants or that might have an illustration that included local flora. She allowed me into her office where books that had to be requested were kept, big books or old books or the single copies of specialist ones. And she showed her true librarian nature, appreciating my need to store my growing orchid record by allowing me use of the library computer.

Tito sent me the database format he used with sections for name, colour and scent data. Some orchids release their scent at night, I presumed to attract a moth pollinator and I wanted to wait in the dusk after supper one night to see for myself.

Lunchtimes, fingers cleaned, I took my orchid bible from the shelf in Cecilia's office and deciphered the Spanish and Latin. I checked for information on flowering period, month and season, which I already knew was approximate. The wild orchids in Na Bolom's garden were rescued from areas where road building had bulldozed away their tree homes, often in the hot lowlands and humid valleys. San Cristobal, in the bowl of the highlands, has a temperate climate, warm and dry in May, hot and rainy in June, chilly and misty in October. Orchids need a dormant period and Na Bolom's flowered when their environment suited them, when humidity and temperature briefly mimicked their original home, some with a rush of blooms triggered by the rainy season.

On the morning the first bud opened, I stood on the path smiling at this golden flower as if I had made it myself, which in a way I felt I had. All those hours and days of watching for the most minute development had produced this. I looked as close up as I could to admire the thick yellow petals and sepals, the blotchy red throat. Now that the bud had opened I could identify it. The listening to Tito, the reading in the library, had led to this moment. Wasn't this exactly what I wanted all those months ago in England, to know what I was doing, to understand something new about plants.

As I was thinking, 'yellow with a carmine red throat, yes, I know it, *Lycaste cruenta* Lindley,' a metallic green insect, as iridescent as a sweetie paper, zoomed in and emerged with a blob of pollen. I marvelled at this instant attraction and Marisol and Emilio, the new guides leading the daily tours at Na Bolom, stopped just in time to see.

'What was that amazing insect?' I asked forgetting that they were from Mexico City. But Marisol immediately replied, 'A bee.'

'A bee! It can't be a bee,' I said rudely, 'It isn't striped.'

'It is a bee.' she said,

'No.' I repeated, 'Bees aren't green.'

'I'm a biologist.' she said.

Overwhelmed by such a perfect use of colour and scent to ensure continuation of the species, I ignored her statement. Marisol looked startled by my conviction and they walked off to check the day's tours.

Notebook entry complete, I moved on, examining the trees to see what else had buds or which orchids were opening up to show parti - coloured petals and speckled lips. 'The long white petals of *Epidendrum parkinsonianum*, are ageing to a dry parchment.' I wrote, and 'new orchids by the library and just outside the garden gate, pale purple with upper petals olive and patterned'.

Manvel and Javier smiled at my growing obsession when they saw me staring into greenery for a sign of flowering. It wasn't easy to track the orchids, they were beautiful when I found them, but often hard to distinguish among the succulent growth of climbing plants, shrubs and fruit trees in a garden crammed with steep terraces, shaded by trees and divided by many paths. I felt such a satisfaction when I recorded another entry in the database. The columns for species, colour, scent day or night and flowering date were beginning to fill.

Every time I passed the new yellow orchid, I stopped to admire it. Manvel joined me, 'Canelita,' he said, 'it smells a little of cinnamon, you can buy them in the market sometimes. People like them.'

I felt shocked at the idea that what I had come to regard as precious was as common as any pretty wild flower picked by locals for seasonal extra cash. But on reflection I was pleased with this information and later added its popular name to the list. Then I remembered another of Tito's commands.

'Manvel, I need some oak compost. Tito says you have good oak mulch in Chamula, can you bring me some?'

Manvel was always amenable and I was often lulled into expecting whatever it was to happen right away. This time it did and within a few days I received a sack of light leafy compost smelling damp and woody. For the next week I created nourishing oak mulch pockets wherever there were suitable trees. Chamulan compost filled in the ledges of tree branches and replenished the bark rafts propped on logs. Orchids, whether identified or not were removed from the bad pine trees and resettled in Tito approved conditions.

Now I knew the distinctive shapes of orchid pseudobulbs, oval and ridged, some small, some long and narrow, others fatter, I worked my way round the garden, an orchid archaeologist, uncovering log nests and bark rafts of plants surviving under piles of dead pine needles. Whoever had made these had put together the essential elements the orchids needed, but it must have been long ago as gradually the debris from trees drifted over them. Soon each plant was clean and cushioned with oak material.

Although my job was to nurture the orchids by providing

everything they needed to make them comfortable and flourishing, in their natural habitats the decomposing bark and leaves played another part. Forest matter contains fungi that is essential to the miniscule seed's germination since such a seed has no food bank to sustain a newly emerging plant.

When I saw seed pods after flowering, I picked off the extras, leaving two for the unlikely chance of germination, and if I opened a pod, it was filled with tiny dots. In the forest proper, the burst pod would fling seeds into bark crevices already lined with rotted bark and fungal food.

Somewhere I saw an advert for an Orchid Garden and persuaded my sofa lounging, cigarette smoking landlady, Carolina, to take a walk to the high end of Real de Guadalupe one sleepy Sunday afternoon. Luckily for me she didn't take the puppy for walks.

The Jardin de Orquideas was housed in a tranquil barrio at the edge of the original colonial town, a barrio that retained some of the grand moorish architecture that the Spanish brought with them. Large houses lined the street, their carved arches and patterned tiles enclosed gardens of lemon trees and hibiscus, just visible through open doors. The entrance to the orchid garden led into a more modest courtyard with hessian screens mounted with drawings and pastel coloured exhortations about our part on the living earth.

'Joy in looking and comprehending is nature's most beautiful gift.'

This Einstein quote was borne out as we walked among the miniature orchid homes of the next courtyard. The Jardin de Orquideas was a Noah's ark for the orchid species. We passed through one micro climate after another, a blossom geography tour, beginning with the terrestrial orchids and the white *Govenia liliacea* that were just coming into flower at this time, moving up into highland forest zone, then mountain cloud forest, down to tropical deciduous, and ending in humid rainforest.

Each polythene mini forest opened into another. The plants sat on bark thrones, healthy white root growth spreading like milky cracks, with clumps of fat pseudobulbs to provide nutrients for this year or next year's flowers. Orchids draped branches high and low, clung to shapely pieces of driftwood, and sat in gourds and coconut shells displaying their loveliness in strange shapes and colour pure or patterned, lilac blushes, orange throats, pink lips, stippled sepals.

Encyclia cochleata lived up to everything flamboyant and weird in the orchid reputation, it had dark almost black stripes and as its name indicates, was shaped like a shell. Sepals were long and drooping. I thought of cochlea, a spiral cavity of the inner ear, and saw the flower of *Encyclia cochleata* as a listening ear with cream earring pendants.

Its local Tzotzil name, translates as 'spook's water receptacle'. Spooks are spiteful demons, not heavily malevolent, but like Shakespearean fairies they need placating. British ancestors were constantly vigilant for fairy attempts to steal a baby, or curdle milk in the dairy, and in the highlands of Chiapas, spooks may carry away a wife or cause the loss of one of the thirteen parts of the soul.

I learnt about the multi faceted soul from Carolina. She worked for a street school for market traders' children. The children came from the mountain villages with their parents and when they weren't acting as stall helpers and minding the babies, they came to school. And like schools everywhere there was the school outing.

Carolina delighted in telling me about the accident. A girl swam in the lake in her woollen skirt, modesty stopped her from taking off the thick handwoven skirt worn by all country girls and women, and she was dragged down by its sodden weight. Carolina saw it all from the cafe above, on one of her regular coffee and cigarette breaks.

'Of course they weren't watching the children properly,' she said of the other teachers. 'The parents were furious and the school had to pay for a healing. You can understand a fright like that would unbalance the girl's soul.'

Children are considered especially vulnerable to losing a part of the soul. Any intense emotion from fear to love can drive out one or more of the thirteen parts, and cause psychic disturbance. Perhaps that's what lovesick means, even to being passionate about a plant.

The orchids in this garden were enchanting but benevolent. Each climate habitat was so ideally arranged for orchid well being, I felt as if I could see these epiphytic plants draw in nourishment from the atmosphere around us, thriving in front of my eyes. I became absorbed into orchid time, even to offering up some part of my own soul.

Carolina gave up on me and the orchids, and I found her sitting at a table examining the cafe menu surrounded by more quotes from Nietzche and Confucius. Herbal teas later we left the orchid garden in the rarified heights of Barrio Guadalupe and sauntered down to our home in the Barrio Mexicanos, denser, livelier, noisier. Our familiar barrio where our neighbour the wood worker's power tools whined until dark, where the taxis parked late and left early, reversing and turning in or out of their small space, the guard dogs barked from roofs, and always people's voices rising above the music of merengue and rancheros on Radio San Cristobal.

In the next few days I looked at my work in Na Bolom's garden. I wanted to use what I saw and felt in the Orchid Garden so that visitors to this garden discovered something for themselves and had a moment of seeing that would stay with them. But I had to find a way of doing that in this much larger space. And I wanted to call on Tito again and have orchid discussions and ask about the green insect. I didn't think to ask at the orchid garden, but someone must have been the expert behind such beautifully arranged habitats and lofty inscriptions.

I had experienced Einstein's 'joy in looking and comprehending' at some new level. But as for following Confucius' reminder, that 'a journey of a thousand miles begins with a single step', my orchid steps had a random quality. Tito would answer my queries and a few days later I called at his house after work.

Tito's garden was tiny compared to Na Bolom, and was a garden rather than the simulated forest courtyards of the Jardin de Orquideas. Neat and crammed with healthy plants, no dead flowers or discoloured leaves hindered their growth, fruit trees shaded salads and flowers while sharp green mind your own business plants spread keeping every bit of soil damp. In the home made greenhouse shelves of orchids flourished, swings of smaller species hung in the open window of a metal workshop and wherever I followed Tito there was another corner shaded by a tree, with a tank of rainwater to provide humidity, and more orchids. They clasped the wooden posts of the house, purple and cream blooms bursting open, sprang from branches by the garden doors, tumbled from holders in the kitchen.

Tito had the advantage of a dedicated assistant, Chalik, who came from Chamula like Manvel, like all the gardeners I met or heard of in San Cristobal. I waited while they planned the day's work and I was as much impressed by the orders Tito gave as by his orchid collection. 'That raft should be more securely tied. And fix that split, draughts ruin the atmosphere.'

Everything was examined, no detail was too small for attention. Chalik ran to perform as I watched. I was envious. Tito saw the whole and the small essential things that made that whole glow with care. The coffee too was made with similar precision. We drank super strength coffee with hot frothy milk from gleaming machines while Tito advised me to spray with rainwater and get water hyacinth roots to cushion ailing specimens, 'usefully they clog up ponds with the mat of root growth so cut a clump,' he said, 'and do the fish a favour.'

I waited for the moment to bring out my orchid bonbons; the green pollinator and the visit to Jardin de Orquideas.

'Tito, there's a new bloom at Na Bolom and I've identified it. It's *Lycaste cruenta* Lindley.'

Tito congratulated me and then I told him about the green insect adding, 'It isn't a bee, is it?'

'It *is* a bee. Exactly that. It's the solitary euglossine bee, a fascinating little creature. You know in doing its job of pollinating it scrapes a waxy substance from the flower and becomes instantly delightfully attractive to another solitary bee.'

I was chastened, my fixed ideas of bees being irredeemably striped brown and gold, dismissed. And my image of myself as someone working in the garden as a helper slipped as well. I observed not only orchid blooms and green bees in Chiapas, but many excellent and well meaning foreigners enthusiastic to offer their skills and experience, implicitly believing they knew better than their Mexican hosts. Here I was falling into the same limiting attitude. I owed Marisol an apology.

I offered my next bonbon. 'I went to the Jardin de Orquideas on Sunday. What a fantastic place.'

Tito stared at me. 'It's completely illegal, that place, the authorities are closing it down. Juan is crazy, he tried to complain about me, and sue me for libel!'

'What do you mean? What's wrong with it?' I asked, confused. Tito explained some of the complicated orchid situation in Mexico and in San Cristobal. But even so I still didn't understand what exactly he objected to in Juan. I did know that Chiapas held the greatest number of orchid varieties out of the many orchids in Mexico, and that it had a huge ecological importance as a region of biodiversity and with its forests and rivers, a major development potential.

And I knew that trees provided a home for orchids to attach themselves to, not as a host in a symbiotic or parasitic way but as a comfortable and convenient perch. Trees shaded the orchids from the burning sun, aided in providing humidity, where there were trees there was condensation, and finally, among other more refined advantages, orchids were safe among woods and forests. Safe, unless these homes were cut down, burnt, turned into grazing land. My thoughts ran on searching for how in all this Juan had trangressed.

'The government owns all orchids.' Tito continued, 'But local people regard them as another wild crop that can be gathered and sold in the market. There are varieties that are sold at certain fiesta times. I don't just go and help myself. Mine are rescued orchids. Pronatura support me, you should go and see the people there. Juan is a renegade. I have permission to create a collection, and soon it will be available for people to see.'

I remembered the times I banged on Tito's door, gone round the side and shouted over the wall and wondered how easy it would be for people to see his collection.

'Yes, Bernardine, so naive. You must see it is all more complicated than some pretty blooms to look at.'

I was disturbed by this unexpected divide between two orchid devotees. Not pretty at all. But was Tito saying that the other orchid garden had been created from illegally gathered plants? The Jardin de Orquideas and Tito's collection were both miracles of ideal conditions knowledgeably and lovingly created. The former by a scientist who believed in promoting man's co operation with the natural world, and the latter by an artist photographer who loved to represent the fabulous and the subtle with rigorous care.

Tito was my mentor, showing me botanically what I could not see for myself. Juan, according to his information displays, placed orchids in the context of environmental politics, and the responsibilities of science. I was curious to meet him and find out about the man and his thinking, what was he like, this Juan who enraged my mentor so. At that moment I wouldn't dare be seen walking up Real de Guadelupe in the direction of the Jardin de Orquideas. I felt inhibited by the vehemence of Tito's response and by the impossibility of keeping it from him if I did meet the orchid rival. San Cristobal was a small and interlocked community. But as the days slid by and my time in Chiapas shortened I wanted to know everything I could.

'All orchid species are protected for the purposes of international commerce under CITES as potentially threatened or endangered in their natural habitat. Many species are protected by both international and national legislation.'
from Associacion Mexicana de Orquideas

When I read this I already understood the passion aroused by these beautiful plants, and therefore their vulnerability to illegal collecting. But it was some time before I returned to Jardin de Orquideas and asked for the man behind the collection. Soft voiced with large dark eyes and black hair, Juan giggled easily. He was a science professor at the state university who wanted to change attitudes. The philosophical quotes signalled his way of making this happen. Hence the garden, bringing people and plants together in his own version of the controlled experiment.

'I like to refer to the idea of responsibility of living. I don't want state support because it changes my way of doing things and I don't want money that comes from Coca Cola or other global companies. My way is to work with campesinos, if they can grow enough orchid flowers, they can sell them rather than whole plants. You don't need specialist knowledge to work in tissue culture, there are new and rapid ways to create plants.'

When he heard I had just returned from Las Guacamayas, the last place in Mexico where scarlet macaws live and breed in the wild, Juan told me about the community near there, Reforma Agraria, where he used to work with a women's co- operative, set up to cultivate orchids for legal sale.

'Bureaucracy only understands that selling orchids is bad and closed it. Yes, they are right when the trade is illegal but harvesting of epiphytes is unstoppable and they sell for as little as 10 pesos a plant which is then sold on to the US via the internet for at least US $15.'

As a part of Na Bolom I made many visits to the woods and forests, with Elisa or with Carlos, to Lacanha, Naha or Metza Bok. I had come to know orchids in their natural setting. It was an intense pleasure to find blooms, notice them camouflaged against leaves or screened by the tree canopy. And as I began to understand their appeal, I kept sightings to myself for fear that the new eco tourist introduced to the richness of the natural world but wanting to touch and take, would be tempted to possess the graceful plants.

In the Lacandon forest, I brushed past an orchid at chest level on the narrow path between cabañas. It seemed obvious once I realised it was there. The large white flower, a purple throat and lip, sheltered under a leaf big enough to act as an umbrella and sunshade by the side of a path we walked several times a day. But no one else noticed. Not even enthusiastic Olga, the glamorous widow from Cuernavaca on her first visit to the wilderness, spied the orchid. Olga so keen on the forest that she made forty round pats of soft anthill clay, used locally to clean and soften skin, and wrapped them in leaves to take home. I paused to look at this pathside orchid when no one else was around.

Listening to Juan, I remembered Olga and her newly awakened excitement about the rainforest and what she saw, how her first reaction was wanting, then taking as much of it as she could. For her, it was the fine earth from anthills, and how innocuous that sounded, a boxful of cleansing mud, leaf wrapped and ready to go.

I felt his frustration over his thwarted efforts. Conservation doesn't happen unless the people who live in the shrinking wilderness have work which gives them a reason to conserve the forest plants. The rainforest is so abundant, so many trees, vines, orchids, birds, animals.

And over the centuries visitors took; took tobacco, mahogany, chicle sap, jaguar skins, eagle feathers, parrots for pets, burial treasure, even the heavy stone carvings of ancient cities.

In Las Guacamayas I was on the equivalent of a busman's holiday, with two friends from San Cristobal. We joined up with a family to hire a local guide and owner of a river launch. As we moved up river, he pointed out an iguana nest, a dryer ring of stones on a bare islet, the curious town dwellers got out to look and one uncovered the eggs and held out a couple for a photo. I watched the guide's dilemma. He didn't want to jeopardise his new but sporadic business by saying 'look, don't touch', but the guide's young helper turned away muttering, 'I don't agree with that, it's no good.'

We had driven to Las Guacamayas, deep in the Montes Azules biosphere, by a rough road and basic bridges, there was no public transport and visitors were still seasonal. The cabañas were more comfortable that those in the Lacandon communities, and urban visitors were more interested in relaxing in the riverside restaurant than understanding the lives of the wild inhabitants.

Mexican fauna is polite, no native creature actively attacks humans, they leave when disturbed too often. Of course, the iguana lays eggs and then leaves as a matter of biology, but too much intrusion and they find somewhere else to lay. Fewer quiet places for nests to bake to the necessary incubation heat equals fewer iguanas, just as the crocodile sunning on the mud submerged and swam away after the launch paused for long enough to seem predatory even to a creature seven foot long, much of it a snout lined with sharp teeth, a muscular tail at the other end.

Having seen the gap between forest life, human, animal and plant, and the outside world I wanted to believe Juan could illuminate the subtle balance of man and nature. 'Why do you love orchids?' I asked, thinking, why not a tree or an animal.

'At university the biology was so formal, very rigid and academic, but the botany teacher asked students to bring a flower the next day and I took an orchid from my grandmother's house, not a Mexican orchid, an orchid from Nepal, *Paphiopedillum insigne*, if you want to know the name. That was how I became a scientist. I observed what was there for the first time and I was captivated by that orchid.'

This made sense to me, captivated as I was, first by seeing the common 'canelita' open from a bud and then visited by its pollinator, the euglossine bee.

The colours were imprinted on my mind, the golden bloom and the metallic green. I remembered too that Juan's first orchid was lilac, a damp mountainy colour, subtle. No one knows why plants in some areas of the world are more likely to be so richly endowed with colour, is it for our benefit, the human species? To entice us into love?

The rainy season had paused. There were a couple of weeks during the wet months, July to September when this happened, and there were weeks when the rain fell in the afternoon, about tea time. The pause was mild and sunny, everything became fresh and green, exhaling damply after weeks of daily torrents. It was a chance to walk in the hills overlooking Na Bolom where Frans Blom excavated a small Mayan site, called Moxviquil. I persuaded Cedric and Helene, French co tenants at Carolina's to walk with me after work. They waited outside the library watching the hummingbirds who came to the bougainvillea every day at 4pm.

We set off to the very end of Avenida Yajalon and the last few houses at Ojo de Agua, named for the spring water that comes fresh out of the earth into a stony bed. It wasn't clear where to ascend the hill but we made our way behind cabins each with a garden and barking dog perched one above another, and aimed for pale patches of stone among the dark trees above us.

It was cool under the trees, the sun hidden and sounds blocked by close trunks and low branches. The oaks were stunted, their roots twisting round outcrops of rock, the earth black with old leaf mould. Groups of white lily orchids shone in the opaque light, *Govenia liliaceae*, earth orchids. The specimens at Na Bolom were not so happy, the garden lacked the cool, damp shade they liked. This slope was truly their element.

We were silent as we laboured up the steep gradient where yellow stone blocks began to stick out of the earth at random. These blocks were shaped by human tools, and must have led Frans Blom to search for a temple or palace site looking over the fertile valley, or guarding the way in to the mountains where the gods live. I skirted what appeared be an old well, the shape looked so regular, it sank deep into the hill but there was no water visible. Huitepec, an extinct volcano on the other side of the town, was a huge water reserve and I wondered how certain hills held water to let out into the bowl of San Cristobal.

Above us the fire break running up and over the hill was no longer defined. We knew Moxviquil was somewhere up there on a lip below the summit and took the firebreak as a guide, but here in among the leafy branches any sign of that cleared swathe had disappeared. The rocks guided us to a plummeting stream which we criss crossed, shoes in hand, using the smooth rock as steps, higher and higher, until we came out to a meadow of long grass and wildflowers humming with insects.

Biscuits and water put us in a picnic mood, Cedric and Helene made a French Impressionist painting, she with her long dress and abundant hair and Cedric in loose white shirt and outline black beard. The sounds mesmerised. Bees and hoverflies made a gentle chorus moving from purple to yellow to pink among the grass seeds. The soil had changed from the black leaf mould to sandy, so perhaps that's why it was open and treeless. Patches of serious digging had thrown up heaps of sand, a quarry for building sand maybe. Or is this it,

Moxviquil, where Frans uncovered the carved head which stood on black velvet in a glass case at Na Bolom.

Cedric shifted an elbow and disturbed a snake, 'Look there, there,' as we tried to see what he saw. A grey snake, a black stripe running horizontally from each eye slid away through grass stalks. As we explored the hillocks and dips another snake lay baking itself on a rock unnoticeable against the speckled lichen until it too uncurled down into a shadowy place.

I wanted to go on and find the right path to an unmistakable Moxviquil, to find something that Frans Blom saw. Frans' image was a shadowy one overwhelmed by Trudi's vibrant imprint on Na Bolom. Doña Bety called him Don Pancho, the name he liked and which made him sound a carefree adventurer but perhaps obscured his true character. He died at the beginning of her long career as an activist, died a disappointed archaeologist and wobbly ex alcoholic but a convert to the forest itself. The Na Bolom I knew was the place and the work Trudi created over so many years, but I thought of Frans every time I visited the library and took a copy of Monteador or Tribes and Temples to read his words and thoughts.

A hand made copy of his sketch map in my hand, I tried to relate the lines to the paths and curves around me, but wherever we were I didn't see what was clear from a distance. Helene and Cedric wanted to go back, they had jewellery to make for tomorrow's market and Cedric had a French class to prepare. Two snakes and ghostly orchids shining in the dark wood had to be enough.

The next time I climbed this far up, the meadow was fenced off with woven branches and barbed wire. I found another open space, a narrow mountain saddle planted with maize and even though I twice persuaded others to accompany me to Moxviquil I never got any further than this hidden plateau. It was never as magical as that first time, as remote, as still. Whatever Frans Blom discovered didn't reveal itself for me. I had to be content with going towards Moxviquil, the climb through the trees, and the season for earth orchids.

There were times when I achieved a break through, with someone's help. Like the time when Carolina interrupted my frustrations about the Jardin de Orquideas being closed and Tito's unavailability. 'It's closed every time I go, so it must mean he's away for weeks,' I moaned. 'And Tito is so maddening, he laughed at my trainers when I said when could I go orchid walking, and anyway it's impossible to make any arrangements with him.'

'He's an artist,' said Carolina impatiently, 'What do you want?' And she picked up the phone, asked for a number, pressed the keys and passed it to me.

'Si? Juan ,' said the voice. In seconds I had an appointment with him in his new garden behind El Arco del Carmen.

In Na Bolom's garden I had to learn that I didn't need others to tell me what to do or praise me for doing it. I chose whatever I did and began regardless and saw where it led. Somehow in this process I didn't grasp a new way of seeing other people. Working well on my own, I allowed myself a spontaneity and trust, and thought that was the only way it worked. It was up to me, the intrepid woman that felt like my rightful state of mind, but like all things fails at times.

I found El Centro del Carmen in a residential neighbourhood with a legacy of gracious houses and walked into a one storey colonial house around a typical enclosed garden. Offices of various organisations occupied long raftered rooms off the wide covered verandah and a poster for the new garden listed its funders, some local names I recognised and small businesses like the gallery near my favourite dairy. So Juan still held out against any state or corporate money allocated, as he believed, as a conscience salve.

Lemon and orange trees stood among flowers in squares bordered by box, and I found the Garden of Epiphytic Plants round the back under the inevitable plastic sheeting. Bromeliads, as well as orchids, were draped or hung gracefully from branches and rocks, pools of water provided humidity and I followed the master of air plants as he talked about his new garden.

'The idea is to change people's way of thinking about forest epiphytes and especially I want the children to know how special these plants are. So they come on school visits but....' he smiled and touched a broken stem 'it's not so easy.'

His dream, he told me, as we walked the enclosure, was for the children to grow up believing that forests were better than fields of cattle.

If the high valley of San Cristobal could show the 20th century changes in one of those speeded up film shots, the forests would recede, sliding up the mountains. But due to Trudi Blom's vision and practical character, then the forests would creep down again in significant enough patches of dark green. She was a vigorous campaigner who started the tree nursery at Na Bolom which was still growing trees for anyone who wanted to plant a wood. Juan was more of an obvious visionary than the bossy, flamboyant Trudi, but he also put his dreams into practice. As I listened to him, I wanted so much for his, like Trudy's, to be reflected in the landscape.

'Symbols are powerful,' he said. 'Think of orchids: diverse in form – interdependent with other organisms – beautiful – and – you must look up to find them. Here, take this.' And he snapped a seed pod from an orchid stem. 'Oncidium leucochilum.'

I took it home with me, the orchid reference said, 'white lips, petals green with violet spots, found in humid oak forests in temperate highlands.' I wrapped the fat green pod in foil, wanting to keep it for as long as possible, knowing I couldn't make the seeds grow, wanting to keep the idea of them fresh.

CHAPTER 8

Transformations

We brush off our sweat, we brush off our water.
Beside You, before You,
Our ten fingers ache, our ten toes ache
Here beside You, here before You'

TZOTZIL INVOCATION BEFORE PLANTING

Back from another stay in the rainforest, I looked forward to my work routine. A human speck in Lacanha's dense enervating rainforest, I had fresh zing in the cool mountain morning and I was keen to look around, play god and create something new in the garden.

Visionary projects balanced practical maintenance. I wanted the garden to look good, look loved and freshly tended. Maintenance involved keeping beds weed free particularly alongside the main paths. The visionary moments made noticeable changes like moving maguey cacti from obscurity under the pine trees and replanting them alongside the archive building. This was satisfying twice over. It stopped people taking off path short cuts and wearing away the steep bank, and they looked stunning there, big yellow and green stripey, twisty shapes set against the faded red ochre walls.

New signs for the medicinal plants, that was what I had in mind this time. Wood and black paint, a brush, these would be somewhere in the tool shed. Cutting suitable pieces and measuring spaces for each letter, painting them the same size and thickness, this kind of making is not a natural talent. If the signs were to be embroidered or cut out and stitched, even knitted up into patterned gloves, or socks with turned heels, yes, once I would have done that. Now I'm more of a peasant than an artisan, steady and persevering at brute labour.

Doña Bety was watering the beds outside the dining room. The flowers by the guest rooms and museum rooms around the main courtyard were her preoccupation. After all my early concern about working alongside her, the visitor areas were her domain, so maybe we would never have worked together. My preferred places were those where Trudy had built up terraces thick with perennials, shrubs and trees many of which were species new or foreign to me. I could ignore Doña Bety, just as she avoided me. Except that in my heart I didn't want that.

'Buenos dias.' I said, hoping that we had some connection, made delicately, over three months passing each other with our watering cans and forks. Doña Bety spoke but I still heard a remnant of resentment, a tiny pleasure in telling me what I would find.

'There you are. You know Fabiola has had some trees cut down. While you were away.'

Was that a rebuke as if I wasn't putting in the hours to my garden work as I should.

'There will be more light. Of course, I remember Trudy planting those trees many years ago.'

I listened, working out the possible sub text as an automatic response to everything she said. Less trees meant less needles, less pine cones, more light but the ambivalence, that familiar old tone in her voice flashed a warning. Still buoyant, I continued, opening the ironwork gate to my part of the garden.

Trees had indeed been felled, and were still there. Pine trunks had fallen across the herb plot, and between them piles of sawdust rose like desert pyramids. The aloe veras were knocked sideways, the plant signs smashed, the very part of the garden I nurtured resembled a war zone. A dead grackle lay nearby, like a signature, black and shiny, ominous.

A delayed reaction made me look for some sign that the tree fellers had tried to avoid plants, had made an effort to lower the 50 foot high firs with ropes and cables. Can you fell trees thoughtfully? When was this arranged? I walked round examining if the damage was irreparable. One tree monster had been sliced up already, the sawdust and chips left to seep its acidic remains into the earth.

I sat on the stone bank under the spiral of life wooden sculpture a Japanese visitor had left in some forgotten ceremony or art in the garden project. I'd never liked the pines, enemies of my orchids, nor the sculpture which occasionally lost a few struts but was annoyingly undamaged by the tree felling. The exact places in the garden, out of an acre, that I had chosen to care for, had been also chosen as the place to allow the trees to fall. No one had warned me. And it was a blow to my gardening progress.

If I was ever to transform myself into what I considered a proper gardener, a capable, serious gardener who understood how plants grew or why they didn't, it would begin here, working in Na Bolom's garden. Since my arrival in March, a warmer Spring than in England but still Spring when plants put on new growth, I had worked a steady week and seen results.

Regular attention, weeding, watering and adding compost to the dye plants and the medicinal plants had made the leaves grow thick and fat and green, prickles grow stronger, stems thicken. I knew the scent of rue and salvia and epazote and coriander intensified as July grew hotter, because I brushed by them every day. If I resented the pine trees for behaving like unwanted and rickety sunshades before I went off with Elisa to Lacanha, I hated them now. Why had Trudy planted so many.

Manvel came up looking downcast, even sorry for me. He stood there and we both stared at the wreckage. Felicia and Meche, the laundry women hurried up to say, 'We told them Bernardine will be devastated, so upset about her lovely plants. All her work.' As they stood looking at the bed, and more concerned, at me, Manvel began to point out all the survivors. I got up and began to follow him, 'See, the tree missed the pitz otz,' he showed me, 'and that one,' he said slashing at the broken bits with his machete, 'that will sprout up again in a few days.'

I wasn't convinced by Manvel's harsh methods of dealing with anything ailing, but the earth here was so rich and good that plants had a resilience that astonished me. 'Even your statue, it's still standing up!' My statue was Diego Rivera, and he was undamaged and upright if a little tipsy looking. I discovered that I was not that devastated. Maybe it was something about not owning the garden in any way. Yes, it looked terrible at first, but I would be pushed into redoing all the signs and how could Javier refuse to cut the wood for them on his bandsaw.

And, heaven, this was about to be transformed into one area free from wretched pine needles, dead brown fingers lying all over the hoed black earth, and giant cones poking up like subversive natural grenades. A pine cone the size of a pineapple even dropped on my head one afternoon as I stood contemplating.

However, I liked all this support and concern from my colleagues. I didn't know they cared. Such a long speech from Manvel and me unusually lost for words. Felicia and Meche followed us. The guest beds lay unmade. Felicia's basket of wet sheets waited on the path. 'Yes, they will recover,' they echoed, 'Don't let it worry you.'

Life!' I said, and they looked relieved and returned to their own work. I went to the tool shed for the broom and the wheelbarrow to scoop up all the sawdust and returned wondering where to begin.

In the library Cecilia put out the orchid book every lunch time and I examined any number of illustrations for size of pseudobulbs and leaf shape. After my picnic in the shade of the verandah I entered the dark cool library, a library that kept to the old rule of quiet study. Cecilia and I complemented each other, she offering practical guidance for company and English conversation in her inner office,

Still too inhibited to speak English, she would laugh and refuse to say more than a phrase in spite of her devotion to attending English classes. I was compelled to speak Spanish. Cecilia had changed her school again and favoured the Oxford School of English. The language school names were classic; my favourite was the Chomsky Language Academy. Someone had wit. Fingers cleaned I took my orchid bible and deciphered the Spanish and Latin.

My working day made a rhythm like saying a rosary and as the rosary has a big bead every so often, inserts of a contrasting prayer, so my day had regular markers. The library lunch punctuated the garden hours and my Spanish lesson emphasised the passage from work to rest. Or at least, like the invocation, my body rested, 'brushes off sweat, fingers and toes ache,' and my brain lurched into activity, gathering more words, more colloquial ways of chatting over supper, a better understanding of people talking to me.

One summer in France I experienced that significant moment of moving from being a language outsider to feeling at home. An epiphany, as Greg, on my first trip to Lacanha described his own transition to fluency. Two friends, were chatting away over lunch, in

French. We sat outside on a Pyrenean hillside eating peach clafoutis, a purple haze sweeping down the lavender fields below and yet I felt like the left out child in the playground and knew in my heart it was up to me, not them. I roused myself to make that double effort to 'join in' and it worked, after that speaking French felt natural. Not perfect but real, and pleasurable.

That was the feeling I wanted with Spanish, a feeling that required body and soul not merely the intellect or the will. However, I learnt French at school in that oldfashioned 'by heart' way. So what was the equivalent 'by heart' way as an adult, an older adult? I hated the belief that age prevented learning a new language, but however much I refused that belief, speaking Spanish didn't happen as rapidly as I wanted.

Gabriel, the tutor allocated to me at the Instituto Jovel, was an amiable, plump, twenty nine year old lawyer with a young fogey air. I asked for conversation as the main focus and so I had to listen and understand as well as find my own words. I told Gabriel about visiting the church of Santo Domingo which I walked past at least twice a day, it was surrounded by the Indian market and I went to Mass there one Sunday, a Mass in the local language, Tztozil.

Singing and faith rose from a full crowd surrounded by the dull shine of gold decoration and drifts of incense smoke. I wasn't up for the length of the service, maybe it was a special saint's day version and I left after an hour. The mass has changed so much since my Catholic childhood but however much the language of worship has changed, I recognised the atmosphere of devotion.

Unlike the grand mustard yellow cathedral on the main plaza this was the most popular church for intercessions. A trio of musicians often played in the side chapel to aid requests to particular saints or give thanks for favours granted. I saw a man in the black tunic of Chamula sprinkle pox with a bunch of basil in front of a saint's statue, San Juan, perhaps, Chamula's patron. I didn't tell Gabriel that I made my own plea to the whole collective of haloed beings for miraculous help with words.

Clearly Gabriel regarded himself a cut above these personal conversations with the saints. He was an urban man descended from the professional or the merchant families, the 'ladinos'. I assumed, perhaps naively, that as an educated and gentle person, and even because he was the boyfriend of Liliana who worked in the office at Na Bolom, that he viewed the Tzotzil as equally Mexican but with their own culture.

Across the table in our little Instituto room Gabriel tipped back his chair,

'You see, the indigenas are fine, friendly, nice when everything's ok but cross one and you find the whole group is your enemy. That's how they are. Not like us who are individuals.'

Thus spoke the lawyer in Gabriel. I wondered why he couldn't find work. But that too was more complicated. I knew from reading La Jornada, described as the Mexican equivalent of The Guardian, that unless you had allies in local politics or business it was hard to get ahead.

'And now there are so many moved from the villages to San Cristobal, the politicians have to court the indigenas. They have come here, thrown out of their community, *expulsados*, because each one has crossed their own group, being converted by the evangelists.'

Expulsados. A terrible word. Such finality. But the numbers of *expulsados* had grown so much that they founded a new community, and built a makeshift suburb surrounding the gracious old Spanish town. On my first visit here ten years before, I heard guitars and hymn singing in a small modern church and met an American woman over a cafe table, here to help build a new village for the converted. Rumour said that the American evangelists were sent to deliberately divide communities.

Perhaps the potential power converts hold is the reason they are no longer forced to leave their communities. If they leave their villages they might not vote PRI, the party in power since the revolution of 1910-20 until 1997 when Vincente Fox led the opposition party, PAN, into government. It was the PRI who broke up the huge estates, destroyed the encomienda system of bonded labour and returned communal land to the original inhabitants, the indigenous that Gabriel spoke of, descendants of the Aztec and Maya. A process that was opposed all the way by the ladinos. Zinacantan, the flower producing village outside San Cristobal received their land in 1940, twenty years post Revolution.

So my Spanish conversation lessons educated me in local understanding. I had to listen when I didn't find words quickly enough for debate or challenge. I became better equipped to join in when supper talk at Na Bolom turned to history or politics, not so often, but occasionally in a dramatic way.

The evening I sat next to Fred was one. Fred, a French journalist, announced he was here to visit the mountain villages and write a story about wife buying - his words - he then asked the young man opposite where he was from. Noé Chan Kin eating the sweet fried plaintain with vegetables and garlicky salad paused to say 'la selva Lacandona'. Although his look said, 'can't you tell.'

He had long hair and wore the traditional white cotton tunic like most of the men from Lacanha and Naha, the two main forest communities. It was such a distinctive and plain look, unlike the embroidered and colourful costumes of other ethnic groups that anyone who visited Na Bolom was assumed to know this dress code at least. After all, Frans and Trudy Blom, were honoured for their passionate support of the rainforest and its inhabitants, and the purpose of Na Bolom was to promote knowledge of the people as well as the Lacandon itself.

Many of the older men and their families stayed here regularly. Na Bolom was a second home, and they were happy to educate foreigners in a friendly way but some of the younger men became impatient. They are such a distinct people within a Mexican world. After all, if the lead singer of a rock group is a Lacandon, (called predictably, Los Jaguares) they hope for more awareness of those who find their way to Na Bolom. Fred compounded all this when he said to Noé, 'Then you must be a Zapatista.'

Noé glowered like a volcano on the brink of erupting. 'They cut down the forest, we protect it,' he snapped.

Fred lost the lead for a moment, as Noé and neighbouring Lacandon diners launched into a strong denunciation of the settlers, land hungry Tzotzil or Tzeltal from other parts of Chiapas who move in to illegally clear trees and build houses. Some of these were indeed Zapatista supporters and their 'communitarios autonomos' were named after revolutionary heroes and displayed signs decorated with rifles.

'It wasn't so long ago we drove some of them off, those settlers. They were so scared, they left everything behind. Not much to leave either. We didn't wait for them to set up for long.'

Someone else was more cautious, 'Whoever did it waved their machetes and burnt out the houses. That gave them the message.'

I knew one of the recent settlements had been violently evicted by an unidentified group of Lacandon. The settlers were unlikely to be zapatistas, more likely to be a group of families taking a chance, or even, Ian told me, professional squatters paid to go in first by caciques, crooked elders, who then took the land over for themselves.

Sharing a meal here was enlivening. I was embarrassed, and grateful to Fred at the same time for rushing in and pushing the conversation to real stuff. It was easy to know the local issues from a distance but not to hear what the participants had to say. Although meals were arranged so strangers had to talk, there were no set places and each person passed the dishes of food to a neighbour, in practice diners tended to join in the language they knew best. Fred had not opted for French or English but chose Spanish.

My contribution was to the next argument about women and bride price, I put forward the idea that since women worked in the home and in the milpa and so contributed to the economy why shouldn't men have to prove their own worth. Women were valuable. If men could save enough for a bride price it demonstrated they worked well, were reliable. I enjoyed this inverted gender argument, taking a leaf from Fred's book to stir things up.

It was also a variation on the 'them and us' thread that ran through some of the long table conversations at dinner. Almost every visitor to Na Bolom had a curiosity about Mexico and its many cultures, and I had listened to many opinions and comments from passing visitors, both foreigners and Mexicans.

A Spanish woman at one end of the spectrum complained how everyone wanted to sell her something and asked me in horror if they weren't snakes in the garden. My spirits lifted when I heard someone take a risk like Fred or talk from a shared perspective, like the evening when Enrique from Lacanha and an American agronomist fell into a discussion about crop rotation and companion planting.

Their conversation sounded like the farming programme I used to watch with my father every Sunday, his preparation for the move from pub to farm, a programme dull to outsiders but rich with shared importance to us. I watched farmers discuss sugar beet prices and wheat harvests while I ate my roast beef dinner and trifle sweet. I felt my morose at times, drinking too much father hesitate over his forkful, worried at conflicting opinions. Even asking, 'What do you think Bee?' because my mother had already gone up for her rest, and she, the farmer's daughter and orchestrator of the grand plan, knew it all anyway.

This was the same Enrique with whom Elisa and I and the student group had stayed, and whose milpa we walked through to the river, a cleared patch selectively burnt to clean and fertilise the ground waiting for the rains to start and the new crop planted.

After that exciting supper, I took my coffee outside to where Doña Bety sat with the taxi driver Juan Carlos. Juan Carlos stepped in when one of the guides or the receptionists were away. He was playing the sad, sweet love songs from Oaxaca on guitar.

'How was your day? You managed to put things right again?'

Was it that melancholy, the soft hearted melody that induced her to ask about my day? And me to reply without defensiveness.

'More or less. It looked very bad at first. Why didn't they tell me?'

'Ah,' she said, 'you should know that by now.'

Noé came to say goodnight, 'So when will we see you in the forest, Doña Bety? '

'Soon, I hope. But you know things are not what they were.'

'My wife is expecting you for a long time.'

She nodded, 'I have to wait until Fabiola sends me.'

I stopped listening and they moved away to talk quietly along the colonnaded walk. A pair of hummingbirds checked the bougainvillea for nectar, and in the last warmth before dark and the mountain chill, they played above the courtyard like love birds. I booked Juan Carlos for five thirty the following morning to drive me to Huitepec. I was going bird watching on an extinct volcano.

Every day in the garden as I hoed beetroot and spinach I became aware of various birds unknown to me. They tried the mounds of composting material for seeds or flower heads and hid in the hedges when the black and white dog came to find any scrap that could possibly be food. Most of the street dogs looked reasonably healthy and a normal size, they ran along in groups as if they had somewhere to go. I suspected most would end up like this one, his stomach shrunken up to raised ribs and yet able to trot along with that steady sense of direction. I saw him every day and longed not to, because I knew then that he would be free of that terrible starvation.

I had arranged to walk up Huitepec with a guide as the birds woke up. The big Russian binoculars were ready and I had already looked at the bird pages of the Ecotravellers Wildlife Guide and my companion obsession to Orchids of Chiapas. Unfortunately, it didn't have every bird I saw, it didn't have the swallow tailed kite in the Lacandon that I saw on the way to Metzabok or the red and black bird that lived in Naha, and that I never identified. It made up for this with line drawings and coloured illustrations of huge numbers of other birds, bats, reptiles, fish and plants.

I looked up the parrot that came to the garden one afternoon and found it was a white fronted parrot although the name doesn't do justice to the red, blue, yellow and green it also flaunted as it sat on top of a dead tree trunk. It made a brilliant apparition, just there, tame, an escapee perhaps and I put up my arm to tempt it. Sidling as far as my hand, it resisted that step further.

Walking anywhere along residential streets in San Cristobal I heard squawks and gentle screechings behind carved doors from parrots and parakeets. They could be seen on perches or in cages through metal courtyard grilles. So many households included one of these brightly coloured, intelligent birds, I liked to believe mainly bred in captivity, that flocks of escaped pets swept round San Cristobal just before dusk. This white fronted one was so clueless, so housebound that it hadn't yet found the runaway community and, also a bit clueless, I called to Javier who immediately wanted to catch it. I foresaw its capture and resale into caged life, a pet, a 'mascota'.

'Don't let's catch it.' I said, 'It will live here in the garden. It can be Na Bolom's parrot.'

The parrot did stay, watching us curiously it crept up and down the trunk and cocked an ear to my blandishments, 'lorrito bonito, bonito lorrito' but it had no intention of being even a free flying mascota, and was gone by the time I put away my tools. I knew that parrots flew in flocks and when I began to look at birds in the way I looked at plants, noticing how they are and not just what they are, I saw the parrots overhead made a pattern, a pair of parrots with other pairs, flying in formation. The white fronted parrot didn't stay, it went to look for a companion, the other half. Other birds appeared on the compost heap and moved on, migrants with head tufts or red striped wings or yellow breasts. I wanted to learn more as I climbed the old volcano Huitepec.

'Buenas noches, see you very soon,' I said to Juan Carlos and before I left I went in through the inner courtyard to the garden. The evening scent enveloped me as I passed the pale blue wall covered with jasmine. I wanted a look at the dye and medicine plots, to reassure myself they were really recovering, that the plants would carry on growing in earth that was bath warm when I pushed my fingers in.

I had trimmed and firmed, cleared the sawdust and transplanted and Manvel had made a remarkable transformation out of the broken giant agave. Cacti produce 'niños', babies, or offsets of new cacti and I had cut these off as neatly as I could a few weeks previously, foolishly in short sleeves. Typical gringa behaviour, over enthusiastic and no sense, said Javier who handed me a shirt and Manvel who produced a bigger and sharper machete. All my brave work had been crushed in the tree felling but now I sat down under the honeysuckle, pulled off one of its trumpets, sucking the nectar as I looked at Manvel's admirable reconstruction work.

The transplanted agave niños looked sturdy and firmly resettled in a built up piece of ground, the earth fine and smooth, the whole arrangement guarded by a half circle of stones, like a green succulent model for a Mayan city state. The babies would do fine now, and Manvel had dug out the broken stump of the destroyed mother plant. Kindness spread in front of me made me weepy, where the destruction had left me numb. Was Manvel telling his family about the day, about the foreign volunteer, up in mountains? He would disappear into his shed entirely, if he knew how much I wanted to hug him and say thank you for making such careful beauty out of the mess.

Often, I was dismayed by the strange combination of plant care and apparent unimportance of looks. Bits of broken glass stuck out of beds freshly mulched with compost and plastic string bound the orchids and bromeliads to trees. This was different and gave me hope for what I wanted.

'It's good compost, everything is organic here, very good.' Manvel would smile, totally satisfied however it looked. But I had plans. Posters said that a neighbourhood compost workshop was to take place in the hall attached to the Barrio Cerillo church. If Fabiola was agreeable, I wanted Manvel and I to go along together. It wasn't my job to ask him, but if Fabiola asked, it would happen. Tonight, gazing at the reconstructed bed, I was happy with our collaboration.

Doña Bety called from the gate, 'Come, if you're ready we'll go together,' taking charge of me since evidently I was still convalescent after the day's shock. We walked down Calle Tapachula together, past the palm tree house where Patricio and various visiting anthropologists stayed, she to visit a friend and me to an early night before a dawn climb on Huitepec.

CHAPTER 9

Huitepec

The bird tour was me and the guide, Javier Gomez. Javier, a young Tzotzil man in baseball cap and jeans, waited outside the hut at the bottom of Huitepec. 'That's where we're going,' he said, looking up towards the steep point of the mountain peak, 'but not to the very top'. As we took the track along the damp bottom to the path up the mountain, he touched my shoulder and I saw a flash of red and black. First thrill.

My binoculars dangled heavily as we began the climb and in the high altitude air my lungs worked hard. I was puffing and moving with effort. We were already 2500 metres or more above sea level and rising. I had been here once before with Fredy Lopez, one of the local artists I'd met through Carolina's fondness for exhibitions and was mortified seeing him bound along while I felt nauseous and out of breath. Today the early morning air was cool and sweet and I soon looked about me and felt it was worth getting up to arrive in the grey pre dawn. Discomfort would pass as I concentrated on what was in front of me.

Huitepec is a small piece of untouched cloud forest and one of the sacred sites for local people. The lower slopes are ancient woodland, and used to be coppiced for building or firewood. Now the pines and eight types of oak have grown multi stemmed trunks and their twisted branches are heavy with lichen and bromeliads, while primitive ferns sprout in the thick layer of humus underfoot.

Even so she was not dull to other hummingbirds. When the day of her marriage arrived, she invited all the birds of the woods and forests, and they gathered around to celebrate the happiness of this little creature in brown.

'Let us each give a present of one of our feathers to make her a beautiful bride,' suggested one of the gorgeously bright birds, a toucan perhaps or a macaw, a manikin or a parrot. Since all the other birds thought this a very good idea and wanted to be generous on this special day, it was agreed.

And so the hummingbird adorned herself magnificently for her marriage. When the god who gave life and colour to the birds, saw the hummingbird in her bridal feathers he allowed her to keep them forever. '

With this in mind, I left Javier in the guide hut at the foot of Huitepec and earthbound walked along the road towards San Cristobal.

CHAPTER 10

Loyalties

At home in the blue and white house in Barrio Mexicanos, Carolina was taking her breakfast; black coffee and cigarettes. The atmosphere was grim, with smoke unfurling from her lips at a rate of knots. I went straight into the kitchen to fortify myself with tea after my early morning on the mountain. The dog lay mournfully outside the back door. Normally, anytime I returned home he bounded up as I opened the front courtyard gate. Staying in my world of birds and colours and names I drank tea and made my packed lunch. Then I dared to ask what was happening.

'That dog, that monster. Plays so rough that the cat's stitches opened and I find her insides hanging out. He has to go.'

I felt guilty for feeling relieved, I wouldn't need to protect my washing any longer and yet Carolina's behaviour towards her 'mascotas' was a burden to me.

'So where is the cat?' I asked, not wanting to know anything but keen to calm things down.

'Back at the vet. You know Loca is only home yesterday from her operation to stop kittens. He says there is a danger of infection, and she was so stressed.'

'He's young and excitable,' I said, automatically defending the too playful pup.

'Too much excitable. He also goes to the vet when there's space, someone else can give him a home,' said Carolina, full of vengeance.

In spite of the growing Mexican fondness for pets, and hence the dual function of vets, if he was put up for re adoption I knew he was destined to become another roof dwelling guard dog, lonely and endlessly barking.

A fierceness burst out of Carolina if crossed by people or pets. It was sudden and alarming, like the time at a music evening when we returned from the bar to find a group had taken 'our' seats. Although I turned to a neighbouring table with vacant chairs, the usurpers were treated to scornful remarks as she stood there, tall and glowering, a goddess of retribution, willing them to understand their transgression and creep away. Fortunately, they were enjoying themselves too much to notice. I had already defected to a free table which seemed just as good a position to see the musicians and where she finally joined me.

Carolina had softened a tiny bit since she started work at the street school. Fearless with her opinions, at work she was willing nevertheless to keep them to herself, unburdening herself to me later. I could only guess this came from the separation from her children. She rarely spoke about them since the first time when I looked at their photo, and when she did, it was with pride but knowledge she was not at the centre of their lives.

There was something about the harshness with which she approached problems that I found painful at one remove, like an echo sounding in my own emotions. I admired Carolina for her courage, and for her forthrightness in spite of the sometimes raw manner of it. I wanted her work with the children, teaching them through games and playfulness, to put balm to her wounds, lighten her disappointments.

My early morning on the mountain and then this reality was my own conflict, making me aware that I could be a better friend to my landlady if I lived elsewhere. Carolina had enriched my life in San Cristobal, showed me I couldn't and didn't want a life completely removed from the rough edges of people, their problems, my problems. At Na Bolom I was in an enclosed world, protected to some extent from normal life. Even there, as my role evolved from a visiting foreigner to a regular with responsibility, I saw the layers and alliances. I saw Fabiola's efforts to balance Na Bolom's primary connection with the *hach winik* with being accountable for a charitable foundation.

At times the lives of my landlady and co tenants pressed in too close and obscured why I was here, my focus must be the garden and the forest. I needed something in between Frans Blom's academic retreat and the tumultuous emotions of the house in Barrio Mexicanos. I had to find somewhere else to live, away from an unmanageable dog, breakfast cigarettes, the French couple's love making in the next room when my bed seemed particularly un-comfortable, the foam mattress extra thin, the quilt unable to warm me.

Arriving late to work after climbing an extinct volcano at dawn and soothing my landlady and her disgraced dog, I needed to put a small patch of the world in order. Some routine weeding to calm my mind before sitting down to paint the new signs with careful but wobbly lettering. I used to wonder why humans weren't designed to eat weeds, in fact we are, and do eat weeds but have cultivated them into bigger and better varieties. Today the wild weeds fulfilled a therapeutic, if sacrificial role, as I systematically uprooted them and laid them on the compost heap.

Manvel was having his 10 o'clock breakfast break in the palm thatch hut, cigarette and tortillas, and not to be disturbed. Various messengers appeared.

'Adriana's been looking for you,' Fidelia said, arms full of stripped guest sheets, 'she's bringing lots of school children to see your plants.'

Was that a warning or a triumphant tone. 'Vamos a ver,' I told myself. Ian hurried by on his way from office to darkroom, pausing to invite me to an *inauguracion* that night. This time it was a contemporary exhibition, photographs of Greenland, the furthest part of this continent.

Then Cecilia appeared to say, 'Bernardine, what are you doing? You haven't been to see me for days. I have no one to help me with my English homework.' I wanted to hide behind a wide banana leaf, the plant Americans call elephant ears, or under a spiky maguey. The 'earth's surface' was far too active.

Cecilia continued, 'Have you seen Megan? You're to be her assistant for the next children's course; Mayan writing. I can show you some books about it when you come to eat your lunch.' It was an order.

I was grateful for Manvel's appearance, he walked past, the man of silence, his presence subduing the chatter. If he spoke it would only be about the garden, he would settle me down like a disturbed plant. We have slipped into a way of, not exactly working together, but collaborating obliquely. There were times when he saw what was needed, showing me how to use a machete as I worked away with a bread knife to separate the cacti, or making repairs to the dye plant bed after the tree felling episode. I've moved on from being a tolerated volunteer.

Manvel has been gardener here since he was fourteen, and has seen other enthusiastic foreigners. No one was going to change his routine even though Fabiola wanted to and that's why she agreed for Manvel to attend the compost workshop with me on Saturday. I was surprised when Manvel himself said, yes. I no longer treated him as my boss, nor needed his attention as I did a few months ago, but I liked having someone to talk plants with, someone to listen. I had a need to put my day's work into words. Today when the women had left he too stopped, looked at my weeding approvingly and I took the chance to ask about the sheep's names.

In Chamula, sheep were never eaten because San Juan, the patron saint of the parish, holds a lamb. Yet, sheep were everywhere, I saw them returning home along the mountain roadsides following women in woollen skirts. Squares of plastic bag covered their muzzles to stop them pausing to browse. Sheep were kept to provide wool for the women's heavy skirts and the men's tunics. They and their owners were indispensable to each other for more than practical reasons.

Sheep were spoken to affectionately as *bikit tok*, little cloud, and believed to catch sadness if the shepherdess was miserable. At times sheep developed a bag of fluid under their chins, a mild medical affliction but considered to be a bag of tears by their loving guardians and indicating the infectious sorrow of someone in the family.

Patricio, my anthropologist friend, told me there was even a ritual to apologise in situations where sheep had been offended. It shouldn't be surprising that animals held in such regard had an identity.

'Is it true, Manvel, that in Chamula sheep have names? '

'Yes, the sheep have names, so they come when you call them,' he explained to such an ignorant enquiry.

'In England the cows used to have names, flower names,' but I didn't know the Spanish for buttercup or daisy, and suddenly English customs seemed bizarre and anthropologically fascinating. Flower names I saw now as sympathetic magic. Named for eating in meadows full of clover, buttercups and daisies, cows were thereby encouraged, put under a spell for enriched milk. And sheep names in the highlands of Chamula?

'What sort of names, Manvel?'

'The day they are born. So when you call Domingo, Sunday, all the ones born on that day know they must come.'

A logical way of naming, nothing bucolic or anthropomorphic but confusing to me. I imagined the age range of the responding sheep or why all the Wednesdays should ignore the call when Mondays or Thursdays ran to their owner.

Manvel sloped off. The men were working together every day, Manvel, Javier and Humberto, potting up tree seedlings, gathering and planting new seeds for the tree nursery. Juniper seed pods like little corrugated nuts were laid out on wire trays so they opened in the sun to let the loose seed fall through the wire into the box below. The three men sat companionably round heaps of fine sieved compost and the tree nursery expanded every day.

As I sat on the concrete bench, lunch and notebook laid out on the matching table, Adriana burst into view. Adriana was, like Elisa, from Mexico City, and had that same fast talking city manner and warm, enthusiastic energy. She was the education person, going into schools to talk about the landscape and why and how we need to care for it, and she ran some of the week long children's summer holiday workshops.

It was often mysterious to me who did what at Na Bolom. Some workers were temporary or didn't necessarily have an office here in the building. Not so long ago at breakfast another volunteer appeared, Anna. I had never heard of her before. She worked from home, helping with the crafts development programme. I thought we were the only volunteers, but maybe someone else would pop up. People appeared and disappeared overnight. Like Marisol and Emilio, dismissed one day and gone the next.

Adriana flapped her arms at me as though I was in a trance to be awakened. 'Bernardina, hola! I'll bring the children over and you can tell them about the plants. They will be delighted to look around and not have to listen to me or do what I tell them all day. There's about twenty under fourteens. What time shall I come?'

I'd have to think up some grammatically correct questions. But, yes, this was what it was all about. 'Give me an hour, Adriana. I need to decide what they'll find interesting.'

Eating my lunch I considered. As I was fixated on the dye and medicine plants, and the plots were restored and looking good with freshly painted name signs, this would be perfect. I could ask the children if they used herbal teas and remedies, which was very likely as 'tea' is generally understood as camomile, verbena, peppermint. Herbal tea was a normal practice. It was only in England that herbal teas needed rediscovering.

I stood behind Humberto watching the men scoop compost into pots push in a seed and place in a row. Javier looked up accepting I wanted his attention and shook his head at the idea of telling the children about the trees. He wanted to leave it to me but I insisted. His refusal so mild mannered that it was hard to insist and put him on the spot in front of Humberto and Manvel. They paused watching us, amused by the idea of Javier as tree expert. Then he distracted me in turn by suggesting I repaint the concrete benches but we ended up making an agreement, I said yes to benches and that I would bring the children over to him later. Neither of us had the ignominy of a refusal. I looked at the bench on my way back and made notes. There were traces of a pattern and colour. Maybe. Paint them dark rose red like Na Bolom's outer walls.

The school children were just like school children anywhere, talking, shushing, giggling, the keen, the dreamy, the bored, and the ones at the back elbowing each other and treading on the flower beds. I did the special trick I learnt from Pepe, the cool guide with pirate headscarf and wrap around shades.

'Guess what colour this makes?' I asked, picking a couple of black berries from the pitz'otz bush, 'who wants to show us?'

Their fingers as well as the piece of paper I gave them stained purple. These tidy, uniformed children were thrilled. Gradually, they joined in telling of family remedies and medical anecdotes as we stood round the herb bed, feverfew for headaches and salvia for steam baths. I had written down questions to give me confidence but it was fine, I was enjoying myself, and so were they. We walked up the terraces to find Javier, playing guess the tree on the way, seeing who found the tiny cerise orchid flowers of *Nagleliela purpurea*. The children arrived at Javier's seed station with pleased, expectant faces.

I introduced him and said briefly what he was doing and they turned to him. Javier responded to the occasion like nothing I had seen in him before, the children were fascinated by the buckets of different seeds, cones and pods, and their attention set him talking. He handed them pine cones and showed the way they open up in the sun, told them how rural communities ask for dozens or hundreds of seedlings to restore the woods around their villages. I stood back and watched the effect these town children were having on him. Humberto and Manvel sat smiling and amazed at their colleague surrounded by children hanging on his words.

Then he led them down to the rows of little saplings and handed one to each child and they stepped back holding the plastic pot like it was the first tree in the world. Adriana jumped in with her camera and a big thank you cheer for Javier rose up. A line of waving green returned down the path and off through the courtyard. I wished Doña Bety was there, and I could say Trudy Blom would be gratified.

The children's garden visit was a success that pleased everyone, from Adriana and Javier to the Directora. It was mentioned in the end of week course presentation when all the children gathered in the main courtyard with their parents, received their certificates and said a few words about what they did during the week.

Watching the children see the plants and seeds and trees as if they had never looked at them before, I wanted to leave something after I was no longer at Na Bolom. Something that would pass on the fascination and bond I felt and that encouraged visitors to be observant, 'see' what they hadn't before just like the children. It wouldn't have the power that came from a man like Javier passing on his knowledge and experience. But it would show why this garden existed, and be a simple guide of how to look.

The orchid database was one part of this, the information plant sheet in English and Spanish was another, and I wanted to write up something about the garden as a whole, from its creation by Trudy to the present, including the children's visit. I lacked the technical skills and access to scan in photographs and arrange text and images, but I began to imagine a garden guide on a wall where visitors would stop and be inspired to look at the garden in a more than casual way. I started to make leaf rubbings with coloured pencils.

Javier must have guessed my thoughts were running away and as I put away tools at the end of the day, he reminded me I was going to repaint the concrete seats. 'There's paint and brushes in the workshop. You can do some tomorrow, if you want.'

I thought about the faint patterns of the original; sharp triangles in contrasting colours and I had a childish worry about templates and going over edges.

The day at Na Bolom wasn't finished yet. Cecilia pulled me into her inner office. She had a small radio on, the sound low and I recognised Megan's voice. An interviewer on Radio San Cristobal was asking her about the Mayan writing workshop, here next week. We heard that by the end of next week we will be able to draw pictograms of our names in ancient Mayan.

As I listened, marvelling at Megan's fluency, a sheet of writing paper lying on the desk showed me exactly how I wanted to paint the benches. No triangles necessary. The logo of Na Bolom headed the paper, an outline of a snarling graceful spotted beast with long black claws. The house of the jaguar will have a jaguar in the garden. Perfect. Everything was feeling very busy.

Cecilia took out books on Mayan writing while I looked into the glass cases arranged on one side of the long library and examined the carved lumps of stone collected by Frans Blom on his archaeological expeditions. The images began to reveal more to me, I knew that some represented syllables set together to make a word. I saw that some of the stone lumps were carvings of people, and some had patterns down one side, and this was the Mayan text. I would learn alongside the children.

I photocopied the jaguar logo blowing it up at the same time. There were pots of the red and yellow ochre, Na Bolom's colours, permanently ready to use as Javier was always fixing or rebuilding some part of the building. I had seen Javier create a new room, complete with windows, plumbing, wiring, in a couple of weeks, and paint it red or yellow so it looked as if it had always been there.

A red bench would be in keeping. Red like the cinnabar that covered the unnamed Mayan princess in her tomb at Palenque, the same red as the background on the palace frescoes at Bonampak. The jaguar against the red reminiscent of why the garden was here, the garden of balom, would complete the repainting, a jaguar, emblem of the Maya and emblem of the Bloms, champions of the wilderness. The red was the easy part. The animal a challenge.

At the end of my work day, a long day, I sat in the courtyard reluctant to go home, watched Patricio wait as Cecilia locked the library door.

'Lucky you in that peaceful house, Patricio. I'm envious. No dogs or cats, just sitting under the palm tree writing up your research.'

'Hey, what's going on here?' he said, 'walk you down the street. Come on. can't be that bad.' They listened to my decision to find an independent home, promised to let me know if they heard of anything.

'Cecilia hears everything that's going on, she's not an information specialist for nothing.' Patricio said as we parted by the market. Cecilia smiled and said this was true, I would not have to wait long. I continued on home trusting that the household had regained its balance since the morning.

On Friday I left the bench and table painted, they looked good against green leaves and spotted orange tiger lilies. The weekend, and I had an appointment to see a house in need of a custodian, a house in Calle Frans Blom.

'The owner is away,' Cecilia had said that lunch time, 'You must get the key from the architect. Here's her address. The owner wants to rent it for a while, cheaply to someone who will keep an eye on the building until he can pay to have the new rooms finished. You see, it suits everyone.' She pressed a card into my hand.

Elisa was already sitting on the door step of a one storey adobe house. I saw it was an old adobe house because chunks of plaster had fallen off the front wall exposing khaki blocks of straw and earth. The western sun shone on the wall, softening its neglect. Inside it was completely dark but the minute I switched on the light I wanted to live there. The main room was big, a big country room, a brick fireplace with the ash still there and a pile of wood, and opposite long shutters and glass doors led onto a terrace. There was a bed in the corner and a table in the middle, bookshelves full of books in Spanish and in English. Everything I needed.

We pushed open the shutters, the kitchen ones and the terrace ones gave on to a huge garden which rose up in a verdant cliff behind the house. Ripples of flowers, chest high, covered the ground, tobacco flowers and cosmos, with marigolds tucked in everywhere, a riot of purple, orange and red with humming birds flicking from flower to flower. Pots of geraniums stood outside the glass doors. A mound of mud, discarded rubble and stacked bricks lay between the terrace and an unfinished modern extension, and I walked on planks across the building site to the bathroom and although the doors and windows were empty openings, it was newly tiled and beautiful. I could sit on the toilet and watch butterflies. I had already seen a monarch settle on a red geranium.

Auspiciously, the agua pura jingle sounded, 'pura, fresca, nectar' it enthused and I rushed to the door and waved at the water truck trundling towards me. A giant size bottle of drinking water later, I connected the gas cylinder for the stove and hot water in the shower, and that was me settled in. Elisa and I sat on the terrace with lemongrass tea and planned our new lives.

There had been a lot of talk about a Zapatista gathering in the mountains, to be attended by sub comandante Marcos, the elusive and charismatic spokesman for the EZLN, the Zapatista National Liberation Army. I had seen his image on tee shirts, eyes showing through the balaclava, pipe sticking out the mouth slit, a strangely avuncular rebel. I didn't know exactly when the gathering would take place and I heard that it was invitation only. Elisa was more interested in her own arrangement to stay at an EZLN village as a human rights observer, but her plans of solidarity in action had been thwarted.

'My awful mother treats me as a child!' she protested, 'Cesar, he stops me from going with him, and now my mother rings the peace office and tells them she forbids it.'

I commiserated and thought how it must seem to a woman in the city, and how in spite of being twenty seven with the courage of ideals, Elisa was still an obedient daughter. My co tenant at Carolina's house, Cedric, found his experience as a human rights observer frustrating. It turned out to consist of watching traffic pass by and noting the number of military patrols, and wondering whether any of the locals wanted him there. I refrained from repeating this. Certain of the rural communities were divided by political loyalties, some inhabitants still adhered to the old revolutionary party PRI and others embraced the new energy and hopeful self help of the EZLN.

We locked up and I went home to the Barrio Mexicanos calling in to the architect's to say, yes, when could I move in. First I had to give Carolina notice. She was more amenable than I expected. 'OK. That's fine. I need room for my children anyway. They're coming to stay for five weeks.'

So the little blue and white house would have been four adults, Carolina, the French couple, me, and three children. The cat was back, resting in peace on a cushion. The dog got rid of. I was glad the move suited us both.

'You look happy already,' I said. 'I've got to go out first thing tomorrow, it's the compost workshop, so I'll move on Sunday.'

CHAPTER 11

Compost and Cohuetes

Weekends were for lazy mornings, but the adobe house with the flowery garden permeated my dreams and I woke ready for my last day. Carolina was also up early making the sounds, happy sounds, of putting this house in order, ready for her visitors. On my way out to the compost workshop, the new keys in my pocket, I saw a big pot of water was already heating on the stove. No young dog accompanied me to the gate, it was almost too peaceful without that enthusiasm. Tomorrow I would be leaving too.

My thoughts turned to Manvel. Was he really willing to leave work to listen to someone telling us what to do. I didn't trust meeting at the workshop venue advertised as next to the parish church of Barrio del Cerillo so I hurried happily to the Na Bolom. However, he was there in the garden as always and put away the mattock and took his jacket.

Manvel was taller than me, said nothing if he had nothing to say but I couldn't walk without feeling obliged to break the silence. With my nervous questions I discovered the name of his wife, Pasquale, and that he had four children and two grandchildren and then we were there, on time, except there was no one else. We hung around waiting, me alert to any indication that Manvel felt sceptical. An hour later we were ten participants in the neighbourhood compost workshop, the organiser had arrived, opened the room, put up the flip chart. Participants and organiser, we awaited the tutor.

It was a typical neighbourhood group from anywhere. I recognised the types from my years as a community garden worker in London. Several keen young women chatted about hens and herbs near the practical looking man who I bet could knock up a compost bin anytime, a couple with a firm belief in neighbourhood values beaming from their faces, an older man who came equipped with leaflets about other forms of recycling, and a man with a limp and a small daughter who knew no group was complete without him.

The poster said each neighbourhood, each barrio, will have a compost workshop as part of an urban recycling initiative. We were Barrio Cerillo, and as well as working in the barrio I was about to live here as well. They all seemed to know each other. Manvel and I shrank into an outsider group of two.

The organiser asked us to say our names and a handsome young man in a leather jacket and cowboy boots arrived to lead the workshop. He introduced himself as Antonio from La Albarrada, a government horticultural project on the outskirts of San Cristobal. We listened and wondered what this cool hombre could tell us. First we told him what we grew; Julio grew maize and flowers, Merit had fruit trees and flowers, Mimi flowers and herbs. Soon there was much discussion on layers of materials; kitchen waste, torn up newspaper, leaves, grass, sawdust, and how hen or even hamster droppings were ideal to make the compost heat up.

Diagrams filled the flip chart pages; what not to put into the compost; cooked food, dog poo or toilet paper, and plastic was condemned – I was impressed when Manvel offered this – a chorus of everyone competing to be the most green and knowledgeable. I asked about pine needles, my personal foe in the plant world and Antonio confirmed this was in the not good list. My frustration with the amount thrown onto Na Bolom's compost was vindicated. I could be happily self righteous.

Manvel and I felt we were in another class. Our compost made several giant heaps at different stages of transformation, dormant monsters lying there untidily decorated with branches, broken bottles and pine cones, slowly digesting pine needles, cabbage stalks, weeds and offering forbidden morsels of cooked remains to itinerant dogs and noisy grackles. I hoped for a transformation to a more orderly layering and hotting up after the morning.

Manvel and I looked at each other when it came to how to make an urban compost bin. The neat little construction, made from two wooden orange boxes, was designed to fit into a corner of a backyard or terrace. Everyone else looked excited.

At the break the organiser served glasses of *oschata*, rice water flavoured with cinnamon, cool and refreshing. As a Tzotzil campesino, the only rural person, Manvel attracted a cluster of people hoping for wise words from a man with knowledge of the soul life of plants, who spent his life outside tending the earth. He told them Trudy Blom made compost at Na Bolom forty years ago when his father was the gardener, and because she believed in it. He told them everything at Na Bolom was organic.

Trudy was indeed a pioneer in conservation at a time it was regarded as an eccentric concept; when around her, new was good and new was herbicides and fertilisers. When the Bloms first arrived, mid 20th century, Na Bolom looked onto farmland with cattle and farm houses, of which my new home was a remnant. One storey terrace homes slowly built up the hill until the former seminary set in nature was enclosed by the lay world.

We trooped outside to the overgrown area at the back of the hall for the practical part of the workshop. And soon we were each nailing our boxes into a two box tower and sharing our contributions to the essential layering, we brought wood ash from the bonfire, and the bins filled up; plant, animal, ash, earth. Antonio showed us one made earlier, lifting up the wooden frame like a magician.

'You see, the bottom is already becoming compost,' and he took a handful of crumbly black stuff and passed it around. We rubbed it between fingers and smelt it and it was good. He raised the bin higher to display the decomposing innards and demonstrate how material could be added while the lowest level was ready.

'But what is best,' he said, 'is to remove the wooden frame, like this,' and with a flourish the stack of composting layers stood there unsupported. 'Place it at one side and move the top layer to the bottom and so on... it will really get hot.'

We moved in like scavengers. Soon there was a row of new compost bins and the original one had been re layered. I saw that every home courtyard would have a wooden crate bin by tonight.

The woman with the hens took me under her wing as I examined some heart shaped leaves on a nearby shrub, they were as big as the page of my A4 exercise book. She told me its name, mumu or hierba santa, sacred herb, and that the leaves are used to wrap tamales, those sustaining parcels of steamed savoury maize, as a tea it is a digestive, and dried makes an insecticide. I pressed the leaf between the pages of my book and we talked about growing vegetables and she said I must visit La Albarrada, where Antonio worked.

I asked Antonio about buying manure. 'Do they have animals at La Albarrada? Where can I get manure?'

He was keen to leave horticulture behind and move on to the rest of the weekend. And I was determined to get manure to activate our somnolent heaps at Na Bolom and handed him a pen. Manvel wasn't going to bring manure from Chamula on his bicycle. Antonio wrote down the address of La Albarrada in my book and I saw my workshop notes were all in Spanish.

I remembered what Greg, the American professor said about a language epiphany, so long ago on my first visit to the rainforest. 'There'll be a time when you just do it, a moment later when you realise you speak Spanish without thinking.' I had listened to Greg and wanted to believe him and as I read my list of ideal compost ingredients; *vegetal de cocina y jardin, poco de tierra, estiercol de gallina, conejos, cenizas de chimenea*, I smiled to see these words for transforming different types of waste were my epiphany.

That Saturday, Barrio Mexicanos, which I was deserting for Barrio el Cerillo, celebrated its fiesta. I was about to leave the warm squash of streets and houses and people and markets below Santo Domingo church where country women in blue satin blouses and black woven skirts sell homegrown coffee, bunches of gladioli and hairy ginger piglets on string tethers, where Mass, well attended, is sung and conducted in Tzotzil. I was moving to the quiet edge of San Cristobal just below the steep rise into the mountain foothills, to a house that was once a farmer's house in the fields.

Barrio Mexicanos was extra crowded and I gave up pushing my way to the white and blue house and stopped to watch lorry floats bearing child cherubs and many blue cloaked virgins preceded by brass bands. Even the cars weaving in and out of the procession paused when men stepped into the road holding up a long stick topped with a canister of gunpowder, and stood lighting the touchpaper and watching as it soared to heaven. The *cohuetero* is first among men and motors.

I had heard several stories about the origin of *cohuetes*; that the noise chased demons away, that the saints loved to hear the sounds of celebration, and the last *cohuete* story was that the Indians wanted to make the Spaniards, so serious in their quest for gold, smile. Everyone around me smiled, each bang echoed in my chest, my heart burst. My demons were chased away.

Sunday, my last day in Carolina's house. Everyone was out. I tidied my room enjoying the sounds of the inner city. Only our house was silent. No dog, cat a sleeping convalescent. I had an overnight bag and one very small suitcase on wheels. It didn't take long to pack.

I met up with Carolina at Bar Revolucion to celebrate our new events; her children's imminent arrival and my house. 'We must keep in touch because there's one thing you have to do for me,' she said, 'make me a compost bin. Promise? Now the dog won't be digging up my plants, I can have composta.'

'Yes, Carolina, I promise you a compost bin and the best compost; organic, organic is good, very good. You can even put your cigarette ends in it.'

It was the full band that night. We asked Roberto, the skinny singer with the zapata moustache, for Brown Eyed Girl, and the bang bang bang of the festive firecrackers made a terrific backing chorus.

Once I had moved into the house on Calle Frans Blom, my behaviour changed. Carolina's embattled attitude to the world, my hard plain room there, the punished dog, all that I had resisted through a busy life. I studied everything Chiapas related and in the evenings I went out to events and to enjoy the cafe life. In my new home the tensions fell away and for a few weeks I went nowhere.

Na Bolom was five minutes walk, and at the end of the day I returned to sit in my own garden, I immediately called it mine. I didn't want to do anything except be in it, idle in it still and silent. Monarch butterflies darted over marigolds and tobacco flowers, peaches fell from the trees and I was too *floja*, as Carolina would say, too lazy, too feeble, to gather them up. My garden stayed wild, and if it rained I put on wellington boots and brushed past shoulder high flowers stepping over wet clay and builders' rubble to reach the bathroom.

When I finally went inside at night, I lay on the bed alongside the fire, sometimes reading, sometimes just allowing the closeness of other people's lives to ebb away. During the last four months I had lived with other people, and wanted to know everything about them and everything about Na Bolom, San Cristobal, the forests. I wasn't interested in reading anything that didn't relate to my life in Mexico.

Now I picked up a novel and let my mind consider other ideas, books set in other worlds than Chiapas littered the table, the chairs, open to keep my place, spines upturned. I relapsed into an almost convalescent solitude.

The one remaining element of my life outside work, was the language lesson. Jorge was my latest tutor and he came to me, private lessons saving both of us money. As I heard the white volkswagen beetle draw up and park, I dragged myself to the door from a post work rest, yawning and with unbrushed hair.

'Come on, Bernardina, wake up. We must work on imperatives and orders. Remember?' I pulled out two chairs and poured water to revive myself. 'You're like a child, so this is my method for kids,' and Jorge flicked a one peso coin before my face making it appear and disappear until I laughed myself into alertness.

My tutor was not only half my age but half my height, but if I was younger and shorter, my pleasure in Jorge, handsome, witty and intelligent, would be shameless. But I wasn't. Instead I take pleasure in good talk, always at whatever age, the best indicator of attraction.

Gradually, friends began to visit, curious to see this house, reluctant to let go of me, and gradually I began to welcome them. Carolina came to pick peaches and gave me a pot of the jam she made, Cecilia called to see how I was coping on my own, bringing me embroidered place mats. Javier mended the hot water connection.

Best of all Elisa brought Cesar and we sat out on the terrace and talked while the air turned from hot to cool, talked about a mutual love of reggae as the dark fell.

'Mighty Diamonds,' I enthused,

'Gregory Isaacs, estupenda,' A litany of our best loved artists.

'I leave Elisa to do the talking, that's why you don't see me with her,' he explained, 'because she has so many friends I am bored to say only trivialities. The important things, that is only for real friendships.'

Elisa fell silent as we talked, fiddled with the CD player she had brought along, she became a listener, an occasional prompter as he spoke of the forest, the old man showing him how to take honey from the bees, the heavy work of carrying water from the river by mule. I saw the spark in him that Elisa found so irresistible.

'I'm a city boy, from San Miguel, coping with long nights without electricity, no lights, no TV, hard work. I ached at night and slept like the logs I tried to cut into planks in the day. Tough. The old guy could do it. Not me.'

Cesar, as usual, was about to leave San Cristobal, and separately and bravely, Elisa was also leaving to further her photography with a course far from San Cristobal and Chiapas. 'You can invite me to stay,' she said, 'now you have a home. And I leave you the music player, to keep for me.'

In the garden I had my own routine as fixed and introverted as Manvel's. Orchids, weeds, transplants occupied me without any dithering. I had my key to the shed, took my packed lunch, and drank tea with Cecilia, entertained a few regular visitors. At night I transformed myself into a clean and hopefully elegant creature to dine and converse in the long dining room while Rogelio greeted me in English and poured my beer.

'Bernardina,' I recognised that throaty voice, 'I'm making a party for my family and friends on Sunday. You want to come, then bring me some more peaches. I need them for a tart.' And Carolina laughed dirtily.

'What are you doing here?' I asked, knowing Carolina was not one for walking far even if it was school holidays and she was entertaining her own children.

'I came to see Doña Bety, and you, too. You must bring the fruit on Saturday, I will make pozole,' she stated.

I'd never tasted pozole, knew it took a day to cook and the maize, bought already prepared still needed hours of soaking and hours of cooking. I'd seen it in the corner restaurant where the preparation and cooking all happened on one side of the same room where the diners waited and salivated. Early in the day round maize, fat and swollen, soaked in a bowl, nothing like maize cobs with their boiled or roasted yellow rows like gold teeth. It was a dish from somewhere else, not a Chiapas dish.

'I shall use pork chopped up,' said Carolina, 'instead of a pig's head. And if you want to, bring some radishes and lettuce on the way and I will show you how to it should look. It will taste better the longer it's on the stove. Be ready for something very good, *super chingon*,' and off she went in a drift of smoke as usual.

Pleased if startled at the party invitation from my severe ex landlady, I agreed to all her requests. I wasn't sure if it was more or less startling that Doña Bety joined me for after supper coffee and said I must call for her and we will take a taxi to Carolina's. Cecilia, always so sharply observant, said, 'Now that Elisa has gone away, Doña Bety will be going to the forest. There's nothing she doesn't know.'

Then Cecilia brought her own invitation, to Zinacantan's Feast of San Lorenzo and I was ready to venture out again beyond my patch to other barrios and other communities knowing my house and my garden were here.

CHAPTER 12

Maize and Pox

'Humans are moulded from white and yellow maize.
They rebel against the gods and so must remain on earth
surrounded by demons.'

Cecilia and I sat in the shady room off a back courtyard, bowls of relish, hot green chili and finely chopped red tomato and onion, before us on a low table. The kneeling girl, plaits tied together out of the way, patted the balls of maize dough and leant forward to lay them on a griddle over a fire on the earth floor. One by one the pile of tortillas grew, she smiled as Cecilia talked to her, and continued patting the plump dough into neat flat rounds.

Juana Martines, our hostess, brought some over to us and we ate the best tortillas in all the months I spent in Mexico, a rich maize yellow, soft and fat, tasty. I knew then why this was the central food in Indian life. Eating it is eating vitality and strength. Sharing it is a bond, especially in the villages like Zinacantan where we were visiting for the fiesta of San Lorenzo, the patron saint of this mountain parish.

In the spread out village communities, and very likely in many town houses, tortillas were homemade every morning. On the outskirts of San Cristobal the better off lived in semi rural comfort and bought their tortillas at the tortilleria. A metal hand flung the machine made circles onto a ledge where the assistant slipped a stack of a dozen or so onto a paper and folded them into a warm package for the customer.

I ate tortillas at Na Bolom, and I ate tortillas in restaurants and cafes. I liked the way they arrived in a small basket wrapped in a cloth, woven cloths, special embroidered cloths and ones decorated like old fashioned pyjama cases, especially to keep the precious food warm and soft. I wanted to eat the essence of Mexico. But I didn't get it. The taste of tortillas didn't seem anything so special. I would have converted with fervour if I had been offered these straight from the fire in Juana Martines' house in Zinacantan at the feast of San Lorenzo.

Maize grew in the roadside milpas with bean plants curling up around the corn stems. The two companionable plants provided an almost perfect diet, having 95% of the protein content of meat or dairy food without the cholesterol and other unhealthy effects. This was what Manvel, my gardening companion, ate for 10 o'clock breakfast. If I needed to ask something urgent enough to interrupt his breakfast, I found him heating tortillas over a little fire in his gardener's hut in the far corner.

Ten o'clock breakfast was a private men's affair, Javier, Gustavo, Humberto and Manvel started work at seven in the morning and the garden shed was their retreat. And there they ate tortillas and maybe beans. Traditionally, wives made them at first light, and men would wake to the slap, slap sound of tortillas made round and thin between the palms of the hands. Whether they were made or bought, they sustained men and women, eaten for breakfast, working lunch and supper.

However, ever since the Spanish Conquistadores arrived, a tortilla and bread divide has existed. Maize equals indigenous and wheat equals ladino and those of 'puro' Spanish descent. This is a Mayan account of how maize came into the world.

Maize was once stored beneath a great mountain of rock. It was discovered there by the soldier ants, they made a tunnel to the secret place beneath the rock and began to carry the grains away on their backs. The fox, always curious about his neighbours' doings, saw the ants with this strange grain and tried some. Soon the other animals and then Man learned of this new food, but only ants could penetrate to the hidden place.

Man called on the rain gods to help. In turn three of the rain gods tried to blast the rock mountain with their thunderbolts. They failed. Then the chief rain god, the eldest and the most powerful, after many refusals, was prevailed upon to try his skill.

First he sent the woodpecker to tap the surface of the rock to find the weakest spot. Then the chief rain god told the woodpecker to take cover under an overhanging ledge while he hurled his mightiest thunderbolt with all his strength against the weak point. The mountain split apart riven open by the mighty bolt. But the disobedient woodpecker stuck out his head and a fragment of rock struck him and blood stained his feathers. So ever since the woodpecker has a red head.

Within the mountain lay exposed a great heap of maize which had been entirely white. The terrific heat of the thunder bolt had charred part of the maize and some ears of maize were slightly burnt, others were discoloured by smoke and some escaped all damage. The result was the four kinds of maize; black, red, yellow and white.

A sick person should only eat white maize, while red maize is said to be tastier but is never used in ceremonial meals. Maize is spoken of with reverence, in rituals it is 'Our Lord's sunbeams and shadows', and is used for divining dreams. The one who receives maize in his night's sleep will become prosperous. Disrespect and ill treatment of maize will be repaid with divine retribution, with hunger and poverty brought down by the lamentations of the maize plant. Its soul will complain to the Earth Lord if a person is too choosy buying maize or burns it or carelessly discards the precious grains. Older people and those who uphold the traditions use maize as a poignant metaphor to describe the erosion of traditions.

'They don't care anymore, their corn just lies scattered.'

Four cobs of maize lay on a grinding stone, four colours, black, red, yellow and white like the story of their origins. A reminder. The colours are linked to the four directions; red for the east and birth, yellow for south and the underworld, white for north and heaven and black for west and death.

The house Cecilia and I were visiting was run by two unmarried sisters. It was rare for women to remain unmarried from choice, and then to be in sole charge of their business. So this was a unique home. The other signs of Zinacantan family life were here; the nieces and nephews going in and out, the framed family photos lining the passage. Also typical of Zinacantan homes, the front courtyard acted as an open air shop. All Zinacantan women wove and embroidered and sold the almost identical results. Table cloths, napkins, hangings, tunics and blouses displayed the local symbols, embroidered in wool or bright silks, flowing foliage, birds and large sunflowers. I knew the home village of many women in San Cristobal by the symbols and colours of their clothes. I admired Juana's blouse covered, as I thought, with blue and green cross stitch embroidery.

'Embroidery? Oh no, it's a lot more work than embroidery, embroidery I sell or wear every day. This is woven and I made it for myself. After all this is our most important day.'

Weaving such fine work was hours of work, I've never been attracted to weaving but I embroidered dresses for my daughters as babies and little children. Even with a few stitches, embroidery adds something of the needlewoman's character. You can move around, take embroidery anywhere but to weave with such tiny patterns must demand that much more of the creator.

I recalled that all the shades on the blue green continuum are *yax* in the language of old Maya and in the language of these mountain villages. Blue-green is the colour of the centre point, a navel, where the 'earth's surface' meets the spiritual world, yax, the colour of plants.

Zinacantan Centre is the main village of the large parish of Zinacantan and its many hamlets and family settlements. The centre of the village is the church, home of the patron saints who mediate between earthly doings and the heavens. Outside in the plaza the church doors of San Lorenzo opened wide. Clusters of women in their best clothes all in the colour of the moment which this year was fir green. They wore little capes and shawls embroidered or woven with flowers unfurling into every inch of cloth, bunches of flowers and baskets of flowers, larger than life size.

The little girls, versions of their mothers and aunts in the same colours and the same embroidery. So much lavish green decoration, offset by wide mustard yellow satin bows on their long plaits and all hovering together, in an all female display, a muted living bunch of leafy blooms. Men's tunics were even more extravagantly fertile, even the red pompoms hanging from the corners and from their neckerchiefs were called flowers, representing the red blossoms of the fire.

Hundreds of people pressed forward to watch the antics of those dressed up as demons, some in patterned clown clothes and others in formal western suits, one in a mask caricaturing an ex president, Salinas Gortari. He had planned to remove the communal title to village land and would forever be a devil man. Two women stood out from this. Different. They leant against the stage where one of the bands played. Men taking part in the ritual performance, danced madly round the plaza, going up to be gulp fed pox from an ever ready bottle, then returning to bait the man with a wooden bull's head who by this time could hardly stagger round in his dutiful task.

The two women were dressed in long skirts like village women but wore lipstick and one had tied her hair up in a pony tail. Attention moved from the drunken performers to the two women. Everyone stared at them in a horrified thrill. Local women stood in festive groups, groups of wives and mothers with children, even the men had their groups. No individualists.

Then these women too began to dance and the onlookers pressed forward and even the possessed dancers began to be distracted. A man in a baggy clown suit striped like Andy Pandy grabbed a hand and pulled one of the dancing women to him. She complied and it was like all my nightmare dancing episodes. She tried to enjoy the rhythm and have some dancing style, but had to hold stiffly back from her partner who heaved from foot to foot trying to clasp her to him.

The singer paused and the woman escaped from her still enthusiastic partner and turned to her friend, continuing to dance in just that exclusive way girl friends do. A circle of pox smashed men hopped and stared, mesmerised by them rather than by the spirit of San Lorenzo.

The two bands with brass and electric guitars made a big sound and a singer danced the length of one stage, smiling flirtatiously at his undemonstrative audience. A smaller group of local musicians on fiddles and flutes made a counterpoint, a minor sound thin and piercingly melancholic, surfacing above the rich chords of popular songs. Each group played unfazed by the others' music, played at the same time within yards of each other, certainly within listening distance. The power of sound enhanced the power of worship. More music equalled more waves of devotion influencing the spirit world and the saints who had elected to make a home here in Zinacantan. Competitive and demanding, San Lorenzo and San Sebastian told their devotees where they wanted their 'house', and if it was provided in the proper way then they consented to occupy it.

The costumed men danced, the two women danced but no one else danced either to the rock band on the lower plaza or to the merengue on the upper that had me moving, and not even to the traditional group crammed into a two tier bandstand. The dense crowds just watched and listened. Among the competing musical styles, mortar blasts added to the multitude of sounds surging to heaven. A row of men sat on low chairs and laid on the ground by each man were a metal pipe and various big bang ingredients. They represented another hierarchy in the range of religious and community duties, cargos that bound Zinacantecos into their version of how the world worked best. That day heaven was inundated with joyful noise.

Being here with Cecilia, I enjoyed the fiesta without being conscious all the time of how I should behave. I was just here, feeling my way into the different levels of the spirit of the place. Cecilia was a practising Catholic and talked about attending events in the church calendar with her mother. Although I never asked her if she was also a believer, Cecilia understood that where religion and ritual was concerned, there was no hurry to move on.

With her as my companion I could spend as much time as I wanted absorbing the sounds and watching the row of men outside the church in the special costumes of their cargo. I could wait for a slow ceremony to get going and Cecilia was accustomed to Mayan time. When it was a question of worldly beliefs, she was more acerbic and critical in her appreciation than me, and a good foil for my lingering idealism, said she had reservations about all those involved in politics.

Inside the church, families sat among a lake of gleaming candles stuck to the floor, praying aloud to the life size saints dressed in their best outfits, lace ruffs and stiff velvet. Mirrors glittered on their breasts to ward off devils. The altars were crowded with flowers. *Tillandsia guatemalensis*, the bromeliad that clings to trees in the pine oak mountain woods, was suspended in articulated lengths of v shaped yellow green blooms. Lengths hung from the roof arches and draped the church columns as if the church was a huge forest shrine. Men in short trousers, ceremonial capes and tunics, played music on violin, pipe and drum.

The saints were reputedly great gossipers, and I imagined them all at a parallel event, a kind of saints' party just up on the next level looking down at their supporters, commenting to each other about the fiesta and the people they must know so well. I sent up a prayer in case I should need their goodwill.

We left to find a coffee stall in the market set up behind the church and the smaller chapel dedicated to Señor Esquipulas. The cafes under canvas had the inevitable chickens roasting away and fairground swing boats drew the children, I bought a bowl of grey brown balls in liquid. I had seen them in big enamel basins in the cathedral plaza of San Cristobal and never had enough curiosity to try. Not pretty like my favourites, crystallised green figs with their sugared crunch and inner juice. The brown lumps were a surprise, plums, soft and delicious, preserved in pox. A small bowl was sufficient to feel nourished, body and soul, with a mellow afterglow.

Pox is the counterpart to maize in liquid form, being a local product, made from sugar cane, and like maize has a religious role. However, as with most intoxicants, its use was a lot more complicated than maize. Or maybe I should say that pox was complex in a different way, after all, maize was subject to all kinds of disturbing modern pressures; subsidised imports from the U.S., genetic modification, the demand for land and conflicts over the use of land.

The word, pox, means medicine. It was the lubricant to open what Aldous Huxley called, 'the doors of perception', and as a ritual drink, pox was always shared, passed round at ceremonies and offered to show the importance of a visit or to aid a negotiation. Pox was not a drink available in shops with a brand label, although there were various types, flavoured with cherries, or the little hog plums, or cinnamon.

Delicious and seductive, pox is drunk from small glasses and thrown back straight into the throat. A strong head is prized, so that Zinacantecos make a connection to the saints and the spiritual world by drinking plenty but not succumbing to unconsciousness. There too the saints and the demon spooks were active and demanded alertness from humans.

'He must drink to see, and yet must have a 'big head' so that his vision will not be blurred, nor his senses lost.'

From the church terrace Cecilia and I watched the firecracker experts, the cargo holders, the musicians, ancient and modern. I looked about for someone of a certain age who might be Robert Laughlin, an American anthropologist. He had observed and listened in this parish for thirty years becoming a fluent enough Tzotzil speaker to make jokes, surely an essential element in any cross cultural bonding.

His record of the intermingled life of Zinacantecos and their patron saints introduced me to everyday Mayan beliefs. I felt a thrill of exploration reading the dreams that crowded the sleep of his informants and friends. The dreams were full of dialogue; saints, spooks, animals and humans all chatting away in a most colloquial and active manner; arguing, fighting, tricking, resolving and promising.

I saw no one who matched my idea of this man. Today was to be a purely Chiapeneco day. Cecilia took me back to the Martines sisters and we sat in the courtyard along with some redundant city guides, their charges returned to San Cristobal, as they worked their way though crates of beer and bottles of brandy. Pox was a bit too indigenous for them, might bring them too closely into the experiences they explained to others.

Some months before the fiesta I tasted pox for the first time. We had climbed the sacred mountain that made a boundary to the west of the parish and descended the other side to thread our way through the fields of red and white chrysanthemums. We finally found a way out of the flower fields, calling out politely as we trespassed through a farmyard, and found ourselves by an adobe and thatch museum of local life. A typical highland house when more and more were made of block and tin with money sent back from migrants in the U.S.

Three women sat at their backstrap looms and chatted, each loom attached to struts under the thatch of the roof. It was their turn, they explained, to be the museum guardians. We were there so long, that one woman left her weaving outside and came in to talk. Cecilia was busy making notes about the costumes, the colours and patterns combined in fine and detailed work. Juana's blouse would fit in well.

There was the life size model of a man dressed as a bull, with his wooden head and horns, and in the middle of the house, an inner room, a household store with objects ranged on a shelf. Maruch opened a bottle of deep pink liquid and offered me a medicine sized glass of cherry flavoured pox. My first taste of the true magic potion. Fruit sweet with a muted fiery taste. I sipped it, reluctant to swallow quickly. Soon we were sitting next door in the second museum house eating lunch, tortillas and beans again, round the fire, talking with the two sisters and their friend.

Weaving runs like the proverbial thread through the long day in between embroidery, looking after children and feeding the extended family. Cecilia took the opportunity to be curious. I think a part of her would like to be married, have children. Maybe she saw the Zinacantecos working alongside each other, husband and wives and children, a harmonious supportive unit, in theory at least. She wanted that for herself but knew, like the Martines sisters, that it had its restrictive side.

'Do your husbands go away to work?' she enquired.

'My husband grows flowers and takes them to Tuxtla.'

'Was it always like that? The men working here in Zinacantan.'

Maruch and her sister exchanged a few words in Tzotzil and explained,

'Our father had to go down the mountain to his milpa, to grow maize and chayote, the best maize grows in the lowland, sometimes he walked down and stayed there for weeks or worked for the ladinos in their fields. There weren't any roads or lorries then. He couldn't come home at night. It was forest, thick forest. Now the fields are all around. Fields of flowers. You can see how many flowers we have.'

The peak we had climbed, in an impulse to turn off the road and follow a path, was as densely wooded as in Maruch's childhood, the ground thick with ferns and flowers. A place with shrines; one at the summit and one alongside the downward path, three tall Mayan crosses dressed with palms and a burnt black fireplace before them, still fulfilling their purpose among the many commercial fields. The means of production has changed but plants still have souls.

Women can be healers and shamans, and perform the rituals at the crosses. Although tradition still restrained women from heading households and thus taking on the roles of approaching other households with the prescribed polite offering of pox. Women rarely got drunk, there wasn't the pressure from taking religious posts. But a few men did get drunk outside the ceremonies; silently, wordlessly, solitarily smashed. It was not approved or accepted, and had terrible consequences, some common to all cultures like violence, stabbings and beating wives. Serious accidents happened particularly burns from falling into the household fire.

Inert bodies appeared every two weeks, pay week. Under the pines on the other side of San Cristobal, a man had collapsed against the dark orange earth, in his case two friends tried to rouse him. Other times I came across a prostrate body anywhere, the corner of a narrow street, on the pavement, in a doorway.

Pox seemed to knock its too devoted adherents to the ground, and pedestrians walked round. Only once I saw a pox stricken man still upright. On a Sunday afternoon driving back along the road towards the town, a man wobbled towards us opening his arms and shouting at us, 'Come on then, kill me!'

Drinking pox was a social activity in a religious frame. Drunkenness wasn't, there were no rowdy groups parading the streets. It was serious individual stupor.

'Only the man who drinks alone is an alcoholic, every bottle must be shared equally by all present – there is no secret discarding of liquor.'

Women wanted sober husbands and fathers and encouraged their men to convert to one or other of the protestant missionary churches. The steady evangelical success didn't completely work. In spite of conversion to a church that forbad alcohol, many men carried on drinking pox without any religious rituals and significance. I counted at least four separate Alcoholics Anonymous centres in the streets leading from the San Cristobal's plaza, one combined with Neurotics. Did the bossy saints invade their dreams and make demands, I wondered? Was that the cause of neurosis? Did the spooks make off with one, or more, parts of the soul?

Dreams were the inner world, the 'real' world where humans met and talked with saints and devils. In dreams one entered the deep world, waking life was merely 'the earth's surface'. Even now I find that beautiful phrase a salutary reminder that life is deeper and richer, if I pay attention, than the daily existence that I see and take part in on 'the earth's surface'.

CHAPTER 13

Land and Liberty

'the zapatista is just a little house, perhaps the smallest,
on a street called 'Mexico', in a barrio called 'Latin America',
in a city called the 'world'.

SUB COMANDANTE MARCOS, EZLN

At supper at Na Bolom, I found myself next to an American on leave
from the military. He didn't feel like an American, he spoke fluent
Spanish, looked Mexican and his body language had that latino stillness
of being. If food was one of my volunteer payments, unexpected
conversations and company came along with it and the long narrow
dining table was designed to make that happen. Inevitably, I asked the
man beside me the usual questions about his stay in San Cristobal and
he told me he was in the US army. My face must have reflected dismay
and curiosity, a few months of war in Iraq and I was not inured to news
of battles and the statistics of death.

'The army has been good for me, I get a college education, and
a well paid job.'

'And why are you here in Chiapas?'

'I have a year off to travel around Latin America.'

I said that was very generous of the army, imagining that it was a
sort of study leave. He continued to be remarkably frank as he passed
the serving dishes of chicken, rice and garden vegetables.

'I also act as a military advisor on Latin America to the US embassies.'

'What does that mean?' I asked, he appeared to be saying that he was an old fashioned CIA man. 'American military advisors in Latin America have a certain record.'

He smiled, 'No, it's not like that. I can explain and interpret regional situations for embassy staff.' And he continued even more disturbingly, 'I'm interested in local politics, particularly the indigenous groups.'

I resisted the implied invitation. Careless words. All the fragments I knew about the Zapatistas rose to my lips, but I said nothing, though I was curious to hear more from him. The nice young man personality, a wife and baby back in the States, his modest demeanour, a man whose job was to tell embassies what the natives thought, this took me aback. I wanted to say, 'those indigenous groups, they do explain their regional situation, they say what they want, loudly and clearly.' But I didn't.

How long ago April seemed when Elisa informed me it was Human Rights Week and that meant free films. 'First you must see the film of Zapata's life, then you will know more about everything that's happening in Mexico now.' It was August and there was a rumour about a Zapatista gathering, I wondered if the pleasant young man was here to know more or if he was moving on to interpret for another U.S. embassy on his Latin American journey.

Elisa and I saw the biopic of Emiliano Zapata at Bar Revolucion. Zapata, the most famous of the leaders of the 1910 Mexican Revolution, fought because he believed that 'the land belongs to those who cultivate it.' He fought so the Revolution would free the peasants from the virtual slave labour system on the haciendas, the big sugar plantations and ranches. The fame of Zapata's slogan, 'land and liberty' still surpasses even his own personal fame. Around the world, the slogan carries meaning for people who have never heard of Emiliano Zapata.

When the rebels defeated the federal troops and Porfirio Diaz, president dictator, left Mexico, Zapata ensured that the return of the communal village lands, the last and worst dispossession, became part of the new government's commitment.

The exact place of his betrayal and shooting was the fortified hacienda of Chinameca. Of the many heroes of the Revolution commemorated in street names and whose faces fluttered on flags for national celebrations, some of whom were also killed for the courage to speak and act for a just world, of these many, Zapata is the most revered. And he remains an inspiration. 'Zapata vive' Zapata lives, is a potent call for justice. The myth, of course there's a myth, says that Zapata did not die but disappeared into the mountains and will ride out on his horse when he hears that call. Ride out on a horse imbued with almost as extraordinary gifts as its owner.

Zapata was from the horseman class, a charro, just above the lowliest field workers and yet with the social mobility of the expert and free spirited cowboy. Because he was acknowledged as one of the best horsemen he had the respect of both landowners and peasants, and in his strategy as a fighter he used the same combination of thought and intuition as he used to guide and collaborate with his mount. What distinguished him above all as a rebel leader, was his rejection of reward and the unswerving insistence on returning the land to the people he represented.

'If I am worth anything it is because the people trust me,' he said when the Revolution appeared to have suceeded and Zapata wanted, not the gradual and pragmatic implementing of reform but immediate proof of action. He was known as 'el tigre' and in the animal world the real tigre, the jaguar, acts so swiftly that it kills in one leap destroying the head, the place of command, and thus halting all resistance.

During the Mexican Revolution a member of parliament said, 'Zapata is no longer a man, he is a symbol'. A symbol alive and powerful in the 21st century. His name taken by a new generation of Mexican revolutionaries, in Chiapas. The Zapatistas. And in that week dedicated to human rights, commemorating a brave man's violent death, I watched a documentary of these recent rebels on a large video screen in an upstairs room at Bar Revolucion. The room was hot with bodies in a small space, the sounds of people talking and the clink of bottles and glasses on trays downstairs faded as we watched the modern Zapatistas march into San Cristobal on New Year's Day, 1994.

They took San Cristobal in a brief military triumph that surprised the town, and left as rapidly as they had arrived. January 1st 1994 was the day the North American Free Trade Agreement, NAFTA, came into force, an agreement that small indigenous farmers did not agree to. Instead they had turned to the EZLN.

In Ocosingo, the next town to be attacked, the army was prepared and news film showed the corpses of rebel farmers, shot in the head, hands roped behind their backs. The Zapatista occupation was over in days rather than weeks but achieved its aim; all of Mexico was shocked into attention. So much so that we saw Ramona, the woman commandant from a Mayan village, invited to speak to the Mexican parliament. Ramona, a small peasant woman, stood on a dais under the Mexican flag and was listened to by the official representatives of all the states of this large country. The image from this documentary that resonated in my mind was a road block, army tanks brought to a halt by a simple barrier of tree trunks, and the words that stayed with me were, 'we carry weapons that aspire to be useless'.

Chiapas is a mixture of the hidden and overt. Sub Comandante Insurgente Marcos, to give his full nombre de guerra, is never seen without his black balaclava, and yet there is a Zapatista shop on Real de Guadelupe, selling boots made in rebel villages and commemorative tee shirts and mugs just like the Arsenal football club shop at Finsbury Park. In my home in Calle Frans Blom I drank tea from an EZLN mug. EZLN being the initials of the formal name, Ejercito Zapatista de Liberacion Nacional, the Zapatista Army of National Liberation, a name much too long to fit round a mug. I found my EZLN mug waiting on the kitchen shelf for the new resident to show solidarity.

In the plaza women sell tiny guerilla dolls complete with rifles and bandoliers of bullets just as the bar where the films were shown is called Bar Revolucion. I couldn't make up my mind whether this was revolutionary tourism or creative resistance. All I knew was that at the beginning of the 21st century, as for the original Zapatistas a century earlier, land was still a hungry, bitter issue.

Between planning my trip to Chiapas and arriving, I listed Rancho Esmeralda as a place I might stay a few days. Somewhere off the road to Palenque, between the highlands of San Cristobal and the hot lowlands, a ranch with horse riding, a sustainable nut plantation, simple lodging, was appealing. However, it was owned and run by an American couple, and one day the Zapatistas arrived, an invasion of small farmers looking for land. The Americans left with what they could carry that night through the darkness. In a minor way this also sent a message that the Zapatistas would reclaim what they considered Mayan land, communal territory, for its indigenous inhabitants.

On my knees in the garden I heard Pepe, the Na Bolom guide, tell a group of visitors about the day Zapatistas, masked and armed, marched into San Cristobal, the old Spanish capital of the state of Chiapas.

'The Zapatistas said they wouldn't touch us. Na Bolom was safe. They knew Trudy was for the same things as them.' Trudy, who had died the preceding year, after an ebullient life demanding respect for the land.

I had seen the iconic photograph, a Mayan woman pushing back the government soldier's rifle in the plaza of San Cristobal, her plaits flying out behind her. The photograph showed a story that began in the

16th century. The same plaza where men bought newspapers and placed their shoes on the shoe shine stool while up in the bandstand trumpets and guitars played 1950s latin swing. And in spite of that photographic image, in spite of the town founded by the conquistadores being reclaimed by modern warriors, the Mexican army took revenge as soon as the rebel peasants having shown what they could do, retired to the forest once more.

The army bombed villages and fear drove people from their homes. In the following years paramilitary groups threatened anyone thought to support the EZLN, and massacred members of Las Abejas, (the bees) a group of christian pacifists at a religious gathering. The film that I watched with Elisa moved from the occupation of San Cristobal and the battle at Ocosingo to show the bodies, men, women and children, piled up in a thatched house in the mountain community of Acteal.

Whenever Pepe led visitors through the garden he explained the significance of the black plastic bags of compost fixed to stakes, with spinach, onions and basil growing from incisions at different levels.

'After the army attacks, people left their villages. We went to the refugee safe areas, and made these, they had no land to grow things there in the camps. They were afraid to go far to gather food, so this was an intensive way of planting.'

These actual events that I watched on film took place in 1994, the winter following my first visit to Mexico and San Cristobal. It was a period when away from the museums and cafes, the atmosphere of repression and fear was palpable. In the summer of 1993 streets after dark were silent. Graffitti spoke of arbitrary killings, torture. This second visit, my months at Na Bolom, took place in a new century. Yet the Zapatistas had survived and grown stronger, though they hadn't secured the control and autonomy they wanted. Every Mexican knew about them. What the Zapatistas did and what Marcos said was scrutinised, talked about, thought about, in spite of a ban on coverage by most of the media.

Human Rights Week was in April and in mid August I wanted to go to Oventik to see and hear for myself what it meant to be a Zapatista a decade on from that sudden armed uprising and two decades on from the beginning of the EZLN in the Chiapas rainforest. Elisa, my companion and guide in these things, was pursuing her photography far away in Mexico City and couldn't tell me what to do. She made an occasional visit to the highlands, appearing in the garden when I was convinced she was settled in the city or was searching for Cesar in a forest somewhere.

'Bernardina! Hola,' And I would hear that unmistakable, teasing amusement, 'Stop so much working. I have things to tell you.'

Once I received a packet with snapshots of objects, with a card that explained, 'these are my dreams, all these things that remind me what I believe.' And there were fantastical arrangements of feathers into wings, or some dried chipotle chiles on a street stall.

If I talked about Elisa to other friends, or to my daughters who were older than her, I wondered what explanation there was for why she and I were such friends, two women, one twenty something and one sixty. Perhaps she was a version of my younger self, impulsive, opinionated and determined to be part of changes in the world, except she had more confidence and was practical. She was my reminder of dreams. But wherever she was I would have to work out my own way to Oventik.

Oventik was one of the five civilian centres set up by the Zapatistas. No one lived there permanently, they were not villages, but each centre provided a meeting place, secondary education, health clinics, a sports field, for a widespread rebel zone, and like the 'autonomous' village communities, Oventik was left alone and cautiously monitored by the army. The government didn't bomb and kill with impunity anymore.

I heard the gathering at Oventik was 'invitation only'. Gloria, a Colombian woman was going, invited by people on the coffee plantations where she was researching rural women at work for her doctoral thesis. Richard, a reporter from the Los Angeles Times talked about going to Oventik over a yogourt and papaya breakfast at Na Bolom. And I felt they knew what they were doing and I didn't.

Someone told me there was a EZLN house the other side of the main plaza and I went a couple of times and pressed the bell next to the dusty signature red star but there was never any answer.

All Friday night I listened to a steady sound of traffic, most nights it was silent by midnight. My predicament came to an end when Josefina, who used to work in the photo archives at Na Bolom, knocked on the door first thing Saturday morning,

'We'll just go, see what happens,' I said, suddenly decisive.

We walked to the minibus compounds around the market and found the right one for the road to Oventik. San Cristobal was full of photographers, not just now but always, and one of them was already seated in the minibus. Josefina, a photographer herself, knew him. We squeezed in, greeting Juan enthusiastically. He would be our passport stamp of authenticity. All the passengers looked the same as any other day, even though the caption on the front page of the national newspaper, La Jornada, said, referring to the Zapatista gathering, 'Today the fiesta of Los Caracoles begins'. The fiesta of the snails, what could that mean?

The article under this mysterious statement went on to explain why the national and state authorities tolerated this event taking place. Baltasar Garzon, a Spanish judge, had been invited as a special guest at Oventik and his presence was as good as an official international peace observer.

San Cristobal is corralled by a ring of old volcanoes. The main highway leads down into the plains, and all other roads are small and winding and lead further into the mountains. The minibus took us along one of these mountain roads, higher and further than I had been before. The landscape was peaceful, cultivated terraces, grassy hillsides, wooded slopes, occasional groups of men, some in traditional short white cotton trousers rolled up like shorts.

A small open truck passed us from the opposite direction. Men, their faces obscured by black balaclavas stood upright in the back. I wondered if we were too late and the conference was over. Then I saw soldiers with machine guns standing on the steps of a roadside shrine under three tall Mayan crosses painted plant green, the colour of the earth's umbilicus. Next to them a giant satellite dish positioned ready to call military reinforcements, or maybe it was a message to us passing by on our way to a rebel celebration. A bold version of 'the medium is the message'. No one commented and the minibus hastened on with all of us squashed together.

We met more trucks and communal taxis unloading people at a farm gate and saw hundreds of people and stalls and huts and flags which flowed downhill in a multicoloured jumble. A man in a black balaclava held a gun in one hand and opened the gate to let us in with the other. 'We're with him,' we said and stayed close behind Juan's blue jean jacket. They were unconcerned.

Josefina and I wandered about staring at all the activity. Women's co-operatives sold embroidered blouses next to health information stalls, book stalls and the new hall for the EZLN civilian centre was honoured with garlands and palm branches. Strings of homemade cut out flags dangled against the freshly sawn planks and a handwritten sign announced this hall would be a health centre, chapel and meeting place for all the rebel villages in this part of Chiapas.

There were the Che Guevara and Zapata murals, expected heroes, but the banners with the name or the picture of Marx and Lenin surprised me. It was easy to assume that all the world had abandoned socialism. Solidarity messages from the Basques emphasised that the international aspect of revolution hadn't disappeared.

Josefina became impatient with this relaxed mood, she wanted some rhetoric, some active rationale for being here, and soon decided to go back to San Cristobal. I bought a black coffee from a stall advertising themselves as organic coffee growers, and watched a woman in the frilly blouse that meant she was from Ocosingo, eating a fat slice of watermelon under a red paisley neckerchief. Like many women here, she wore it across her face, cowboy style. These women were 21st century 'Adelitas', the women who went to war alongside Zapata's men in flounced skirts and shawls, draped with bandoliers of bullets, rifles in hand.

Women are prominent in the EZLN. They are comandantes as well as the men; like comandantes Ramona and Esther, the former signing the San Andres Accord in 1996 which brought hope and the promise of indigenous autonomy, later watered down and finally rejected both by the house of representatives and the Zapatistas.

After the angst of getting here I needed a speech or two myself, or at least for someone to tell me if there would be some. I couldn't see any organised event and approached the men on a bookstall. 'When are the speeches?' I asked, 'and where's Marcos?' They smiled indulgently and said 'later' and that Marcos had been prevented from attending because of stomach pain.

So I made my way down to a football pitch with a covered stand and sat with my coffee. It was a front row view of a kickabout where some of the players were masked others not. All around me were picnicking groups, families, women and children, men. An orderly file marched off and I wondered if something was happening but a while later they reappeared each carrying a small stack of freshly made tortillas. A loudspeaker broadcast a reminder to clear up after eating, Oventik was for everyone and everyone needed to take care of it.

Besides the stand and the new hall, the only other permanent building was a two storey concrete block. Hanging out of one window a banner declared,

‘*Somos chingo* (we're screwed)
Somos desmadre (we're messed up)
ya basta!’ (that's enough)

Maybe this was where Elisa came for her political weekend listening to speakers from the rebel villages by day, sharing ideas, experiences and cigarettes by night. She saw 'the man' as she called Marcos, 'him'. Wanting to tell me but not wanting others to hear and understand.

The boy eating his tortillas on the bench next to me explained that the building was a secondary school and the Italian supporters were staying there and that was their banner. I asked him what *aguascalientes* and *caracoles* meant. I only knew that the *caracoles* stage had just been initiated, that this was a sort of launch fiesta.

'It's the time of caracoles now, is that right? But what does it signify, snails?'

He took my hand and clasped it sideways, curving his fingers in mine. Mine responded naturally and curved round his. I smiled, it's the spiral of a snail shell.

'That is the meaning,' he said. 'From the inside to outside and from outside to inside. And you make that snail by joining hands. This place, Oventik, is where we join together.'

Right. Now I understood. And encouraged I tried to decipher the previous stage, *aguascalientes*, which means literally, hot waters. In my mind I had interpreted it as the coming to the boil of the EZLN, its creation. The boy laughed.

'No. It's a place, the name of where Zapata met with two others and agreed to start the Mexican Revolution. Aguascalientes is a town.'

Hot water and snails. I wouldn't forget that.

As I wrote this book a year after the *fiesta de los caracoles*, on the tenth anniversary of the Zapatista insurrection in Chiapas and the twentieth anniversary of the founding of the EZLN, sub comandante Marcos issued an invitation to Inter Milan football club to take part in a 'galactic match', the trophy to be, not a silver cup but a *pozol*. A *pozol* is the clay pot used for cooking. Marcos would take the role of 'Head Coach'. I like to imagine that boy as one of the team.

Marcos is a brilliant publicist, knowing exactly how to draw attention and yet avoid personal scrutiny. Just as when I expressed sadness at the image of men carrying wooden guns as they marched out of the forest and into San Cristobal twelve years ago, Elisa's boyfriend, Cesar had waved away my concern, explaining, 'But that's so Mayan. Who's going to shoot men with wooden guns.' But then there were the men, hands tied, with red flowers spreading through their hair, petals of blood strewn along the street.

Marcos' stomach pain, it turned out later, was not because of his anti-personality cult attitude, as Josefina put it, but due to 'laughing so much' at the media furore and politicians' alarm at the idea of indigenous people getting together. In spite of the ban on media coverage, the national flurry of discussion about why the conference was happening and what it all meant was sufficient; Marcos didn't need to do or say anything. He didn't need to be there. People came to see Marcos and saw not him but small farmers, women and children, coffee workers, local leaders, market traders, co-operatives, health workers, saw them exchanging information, eating, talking, playing football. And the Zapatistas themselves saw how many they are, and that no *estan solos*. They are not alone. The boy said he came from a village where some were Zapatistas and some Priistas, the latter supported the party, PRI, brought into being by the original revolution. In one of his manifestos, Marcos described how land reform was put into practice, often many years after the Revolution, in his own inimitable way, sending it addressed from the Lacandon forest, where he was as elusive as the jaguar.

'The good and level land for the estate owners; rocky ground and hills for the indigenous. That is the PRI agrarian reform.'

Like the land, so many other things came in poor quality parcels. Jorge, my favourite language tutor, who loved to relate entertaining stories while educating me, told me about teaching in an indigenous village where there was no electricity and the teacher's only place to make a bed was on the classroom tables above the damp floor, surrounded by croaking frogs.

My companion finished his tortillas and our conversation; we joined hands again to say goodbye, and wished each other good luck. I bought my son a tee shirt with Emiliano Zapata on the front, a Zapata with blue wings and accompanied by naked cherubs in balaclavas. The slogan said, Independent Rebel Secondary School. My son was thirty years old, so maybe a tee shirt with the word 'school', even in Spanish, was out, but I wouldn't buy a tee shirt decorated with guns.

Since no one was going to make speeches and the atmosphere was of festivities coming to an end – several people had taken notice of the request to pick up litter – I made my way back to the gate. Cars, taxis and minibuses were filling up, a small truck gleaming with chrome drew near and I stepped up, handing the driver my 16 pesos fare.

The men clambered onto the cab roof and sat there singing. The rest of us remained holding onto the wooden side slats, standing close together, warm, lively, standing together just like the song and as we passed groups of people walking or waiting by the road a shout rang from the cab roof. Hands punched the air and they carried on singing, black hair streaming in the backdraft. I waved along with the rest of us packed in the back. Most of the walkers smiled and waved, some looked surprised at this raucous display.

The Zapatistas I saw at the gathering were quiet, or anonymous behind their kerchiefs and balaclavas. They had more to lose, more to be reserved about. We were townies returning to safety. The soldiers and the satellite were gone. All this solidarity and joy in a truck moving along a mountain road competed with an insidious feeling of why didn't we get there earlier.

The next afternoon Josefina called round for our promised walk by the river. Before reaching the edge of town, we passed cafe terraces lined with white plastic tables and chairs, where big family parties lingered over Sunday lunch, or couples jigged and waltzed to the live brass and guitar groups. Their signs hung in every street, Five Star Big Band or Ritmos Latino, waving at me on my daily walks from Na Bolom into town, open doors showed drum kits stacked up in tiny rooms, or men practising. I wondered then where they all played and now I knew it wasn't only mariachi serenades like the time I woke at 5 am and heard love songs next door for Mothers Day.

As we walked, Josefina complained about the Zapatista gathering, 'so boring, no speeches, no Marcos. If it hadn't been for meeting Juan it would have been a wasted trip. Gloria says the same thing, she can't think why the coffee co-op asked her.' But I had heard already that the speeches, the talk about the future, began the day early, farmer time.

We crossed the road that encircled San Cristobal to the pine woods and wandered among the reserve named for Trudy in her maiden name, Reserva Trudy Duby. A friend and benefactor bought this wooded valley in the lower slopes of the mountains to celebrate Trudy's passion to keep trees safe. In spite of the inevitable raids for fuel, it was dense with mature pines. I looked down into a dark green mass and across the valley to the jagged ex volcanoes where little groups of block houses and maize fields at impossible angles crept up the mountains, clearing the wilderness in their way.

The EZLN was founded on rural issues, the continual struggle over land and ownership and a history of using natural resources as if they were infinite. The Lacandons' hostility to the peasant farmer and the Zapatistas, was based on the movement of landless farmers in the

20th century into the rainforest, when the government saw it as a great unused territory.

Fabiola said that the reason the area around San Cristobal still had so many trees was mainly because of Trudy and the tree nursery she set up at Na Bolom so many years ago, fifty years ago, when few people thought the abundance of woodland could disappear so rapidly. From this reserve in her name I saw what she imagined. Here in the highlands it's a constant struggle between the need for wood for cooking, land for food, and the benefits of mature mixed woodlands, holding the topsoil steady, making clean air and good earth from the annual laying down of leaves and undergrowth. This wasn't hurricane country like the neighbouring state, Yucatan, but the abnormal strength and number of recent hurricanes there has enhanced the rainy season in Chiapas. Rain and denuded slopes add up to soil erosion and from this the destruction of homes and livelihoods.

Thank god for the sacred mountain I could see on the opposite side of San Cristobal, the boundary of Zinacantan. Home for the master of storms, the only human marks were the pathways leading through the trees to his shrines. The sacred mountain, where part of the human soul went each night. So many reasons to protect the woods.

I did get to see Marcos. Elisa no longer appeared in San Cristobal but an occasional email arrived. Cesar, the anarchist lover was mentioned less and less.

I was the one who missed news of him since he and I found a mutual passion for Jamaican music over a bottle of wine on the terrace of the house in Calle Frans Blom but Elisa has flown this Mayan mountain land, and Cesar, into a wider world. She and I coincided once more, in the capital, Mexico City, and made our way to another mountain and a smaller gathering where Marcos was present as the honoured guest. Before I also left Chiapas, Elisa became one of the regular photographers for the EZLN. 'Bernardina,' she wrote, 'I don't know what this can do but I know it's history and I want to be here.'

'Somos chingo
Somos desmadre
ya basta!'

CHAPTER 14

Naha

What cheers is the end of a mule heading for the bush'

Frans Blom

Heading for the bush cheered me too, but it was no longer by mule. Mule might have been more reliable than the white van that broke down between Naha and Metza Bok on our last trip down into the Lacandon forest. Broke down on the roughest road I had travelled, a road with lumps of rock and holes like wells. The van died in the hottest part of the day, opposite a cluster of cattle herders' homes, and we spent four hours waiting for a lift in a windowless shop drinking coke among sacks of rice and chicken feed.

Outside the open door men passed by on sauntering horses or sat under a tree as unmoving and dramatically posed as a cowboy film still. Eight year old Bor, allowed to come with us on a special trip, stood by the door in his grubby white tunic and stared disapprovingly at these settlers. Bored at last, he came to sit with me then fell sweatily asleep, head on my lap.

In spite of this breakdown moment, I had a need to get back to the forest once more. Naha in particular, further and deeper into the forest than Lacanha, had something about it that I loved. Maybe it was sleeping in the open air surrounded by the trees, and then there was something about the people I knew there. In Lacanha brothers didn't speak to each other, and in Metza Bok, a tiny community too small to be viable without outside support, we arrived midday to find all the men silently drunk, each in his own home.

This time a sleek new van was prepared for its first run, already toasted by the entire staff in tiny measures of champagne. No chance of breakdowns. At seven the next morning we loaded camp supplies, and boxes of donated school materials; paper, pencils and colouring books. Giant packets of animalitos, little biscuit shapes of cats, fish, birds and tigers for the children filled any spaces. We set off and my ears popped as we descended from the highlands. Fabiola, Ian, Doña Bety and me. Doña Bety and I in the back seats with a rare view of Ian and Fabiola together.

We arrived in Naha after sunset. It was completely dark, no light shone from any of the cabins. As we pulled up to get the pots and pans and hammocks stored at Chan Kin Cuarto's house a myriad of little lamps moved towards us. Men with headbands each set with a flat torch, clustered around us like a flock of cheerful fireflies. We were their fresh supply of live entertainment, and they looked especially pleased to see that Fabiola, the directora, had come to visit.

Back in the van with our household gear we drove on to the camp, still the same place where a fifteen year old Bety helped Trudy and Don Pancho, set up camp. A couple of hundred yards through the trees the two open sided shelters stood in a grassy clearing surrounded by the forest. Some of the boys ran behind us and a couple cycled before, their white tunics dim flutters in the darkness.

We put the hammocks up under the thatched sleeping area and I unrolled my sleeping bag and found leggings and a long sleeved tee shirt by the light of the gas lamp that Ian had already lit. I was prepared for the night time cold this time, Naha is high up. The fire lit and a pot of water boiled, Fabiola opened the big box of trainers provided by a supporter of Na Bolom and a great trying on by the boys began. Fabiola pulled out a giant pair specially bought in Mexico City in the hope that these would fit Juanito, a man with particularly large feet, and gave them to one of his neighbours. The boys left, a few adults arrived, and finally the camp in the forest settled into silence and sleep.

The sound of whistling woke us. It was Juanito's way of letting us know he had come to visit. He waited as no one wanted to get up just yet. Ian and Fabiola had a tent and the zipper stayed done up. I kept the sleeping bag up to my eyes. But it wasn't long before the snap and crackle of wood told me Doña Bety was busy and had the fire going. I swung my legs over the hammock side, rummaged for my towel and toothbrush and went down to the stream picking up a bucket on the way.

Toucans flew out of the tree above me as I stepped into the shallow water. I scooped water for teeth cleaning and a wash. Trees and vines were all I saw, I became Eve as I poured water over my body and clean and smooth I stayed there without moving to listen to the sounds of the forest, the fall of a branch, the bird calls and the raspings and tickings of a million insects. I slung my bucket of soapy foot rinse on the earth. We were very particular about soap and keeping streams pure. Dried and clothed I returned to civilization, my bucket full of fresh water.

Juanito was as tousled as ever, a big shambling man in a worn shift but sparkling new footwear. He showed me how well the trainers fitted as I poured hot water onto tea bags. Doña Bety was already cooking breakfast and soon the table filled up with men and boys delighted to have visitors. I handed out the plates of eggs and tortillas making sure Fabiola got to eat while she talked to elderly Don Antonio. The table took up most of the long shelter, the square fire platform and shelves for pots and washing up bowls filled the opposite end. It was this domestic end where the girls and a few young women with babies in slings gathered regarding all the excitement. Doña Bety knew exactly who was related to whom and her enquiries on mothers and cousins drew them into conversation. They were shy compared to their brothers.

I rarely spent much time with Fabiola or Ian, at Na Bolom I was in the garden, or the library and the dining room. They were tucked away in their respective rooms. The office and the archives left behind in San Cristobal, I saw them relax. Their indoor pallor made them distinctive; Ian and Fabiola were white as milk, as white as the moon. My arms, face and the tee shirt v of my chest were brown, not a suntan but a weathered colour made from sun, wind and rain, I had grown more like the colour of Manvel, the brown of old oak leaves.

Ian as the archivist for Trudy's photographs, spent hours in the darkroom. At Na Bolom, he had a preoccupied air which kept people guessing his thoughts, and his voice was always low as if he didn't want to give anything away. Fabiola was more often on the phone than out among trees, although the Lacandon was the inspiration for Na Bolom's existence. Here in Naha, it was as if they had emerged from hibernation, and their hearts and minds seemed to warm up and glow. When I saw Fabiola reach for Ian's hand and the half smile he gave her it became a whole honeymoon of feeling.

The revelation came when the games started. Most of Naha's adults had disappeared to pursue their daily life, saying *ko'ox* or *bin in kah*, let's go or I'm going. Fabiola brought out balloons for the children and soon there was much puffing and tying.

'Put your balloons like this,' she ordered, holding one behind her. 'Look at us,' and I was manoeuvred into position, my back to the balloon so we became conjoined twins.

This was copied enthusiastically and then pairs of boys raced, each pair back to back, a balloon between their shoulders. There must have been about two dozen boys under twelve, most with long black hair and fringes, barefoot or in the new trainers, all running and laughing and shouting like a school sports day, except we were surrounded and shaded by trees 40 metres tall. Chachalaca birds cackled in protest as they retreated deeper into the forest.

My contribution was a three legged race which Fabiola and I demonstrated remarkably gracefully. It was my speciality, I had won many parent and child races, and knew the secret of perfect co-ordination was counting. One - two, one - two, I said as our joined feet came down followed evenly by each single foot. When the boys attempted this, the result was a pile up. The balloon competitions were more manageable, and new back to back ones soon initiated. This Fabiola I marvelled at, playful and relaxed, a natural with the children.

While Fabiola was surrounded by balloons and boys, I entertained Bor, Chan Kin Cuarto's youngest son, and my companion on the way to Metza Bok. He was a sturdy little boy with fair hair, and reminded me of my eldest grandson. They were the same age and both had round faces and similar colouring, white skin and blond hair but Bor, like his two older brothers was albino. Because of this, his eyesight was poor. He didn't join in with the other boisterous children, but he was still mad keen for games and so we played a version of volley ball together, whacking a green balloon up into the air.

The girls spread out to the table, it had become an informal cafe with mugs of hot chocolate and plates of biscuits. The younger girls used the paper and crayons we brought, the older ones chatted or helped Doña Bety round the fire. Ian took a few photographs but left the children to Fabi. I avoided talking English with him, but this only emphasised that Ian wasn't an enthusiastic talker.

The next day Fabiola reverted to her official role when we took the boxes of supplies to the school and she made a presentation. The schoolroom was at the furthest point of the village and we drove there past cabins, some made from wood and palm thatch, a few of breeze block. Hibiscus hedges made pretty boundaries. The school was crowded with men, a few with short hair, most in Naha style, long with a fringe. There were few children and no teacher as it was the long summer holiday. In term teachers travelled in from towns to teach in the forest communities, stayed for the week and returned home at weekends.

Every community we passed had a school but I also knew that the teacher didn't always arrive, and as a profession teachers had a belligerent reputation. In town I saw a strike on the televison news, a strike so violent that it was more like a prison drama, with men on school roofs hurling bricks and police in riot gear hustling teachers into vans.

Fabiola stood on the teacher's dais, made a short speech and handed over the boxes of school materials. The mood was amiable and relaxed, a gathering of men in spotless white, extras for some angelic production. A few jokes and handshakes followed then people dispersed or chatted. I recognised several, Chan Kin Cuarto who rented out a room (cuarto) to visitors and Don Antonio from my regular meeting place, the dining table at Na Bolom. Don Antonio was shrinking into old age and a little deaf but I could still see the curly moustached handsome former suitor to a teenage Doña Bety. And there was Juanito, epileptic and unmarried, consequently the tendency to be unwashed and unbrushed. New shoes had revived him and gave him a proud confidence.

Doña Bety seemed reluctant to introduce me to the man I wanted to meet, Atanasio, saying that he was bound to come to the camp later on. This was not the Atanasio of Lacanha, the depressed man who wove the basket I bought, once Elisa had bargained his asking price upward. This Naha Atanasio had a reputation for plant knowledge, and a reputation for reserve. He lived further into the forest away from the long scatter of cabins by the airstrip.

My playmate Bor's two brothers appeared, Chan Kin and Kayum, and I asked them to point him out. I knew how easy it was to get put off what I wanted to do, I needed other people's help or advice. In Naha it would be impossible to explore far on my own, there were few paths or tracks away from the white crushed rock road and the grass expanse between homes, part runway for small planes and part village green. I could set off but might never find my way back.

I wanted to get in among the trees and walk with someone I could ask about what I saw, someone I could listen to. I had heard that Atanasio not only knew the plants but had an interest in their uses, whereas so many Lacandones had other preoccupations. When I found him and asked if he would take me into the forest to look at plants, he didn't look keen but I persevered and he said to come the next morning when it was still cool.

In the early grey light, I left the camp and walked out of the trees to the empty road, a white scar in the green. Atanasio's house sat between the road and the lake. It wasn't a house proper, but several cabins made of wood plank or bamboo, with roofs of palm thatch or corrugated tin. Chickens ran about, a dog barked and Atanasio appeared. He looked rather reserved still, as if he regretted yesterday's agreement.

First he sat on a chair in the shade of an overhanging roof and pointed out herbs growing randomly by flattened earth paths between cabins. I found a large stone for a seat and crouched on it, arms clasping my knees.

'You know what that one is for? It's for cleansing the stomach. And this we use in cooking.'

Basil and epazote I knew well from Na Bolom's garden and could offer their names but I was pleased Atanasio took this seriously enough to start explaining their properties. He seemed reassured by this exchange as if we had introduced our true selves.

'Down to the lake or into the forest?'

I chose the forest. It was all forest but the vegetation was lower and more open towards the lake and I wanted to feel enclosed. Soon we turned off into the trees and started to climb up. The density obscured a hilly terrain and I used my hands to grasp branches to steady myself and keep up with his pace. He stopped and picked a leaf.

'This is sakan, the root is good for snakebite. I've used it against nauyaca.' I looked at his wellington boots and regretted my choice of trainers.

'Here I was bitten and another time here.' He tapped each of his ankles and smiled without any guile. 'This is the part to use.' And he pulled up a piece of root from the loose leaf mould, scraped away the skin and invited me to eat a piece. I tasted it, a dry bitter, not the same taste as a blackthorn sloe but it made the same saliva inhibiting pucker to my mouth. He pulled some long thin leaves from a branch, and held out his open hand so I could look closely, as I balanced notebook and pencil, 'You make a tea with these leaves and it stops dysentery.'

Atanasio told me the names, some in Spanish and when he didn't know the name in Spanish, in Maya. The words were equally foreign to me and I couldn't always work out how to write them but the Mayan names, short, hard sounds, were easier to write phonetically and made sense for reading later. The dysentery cure I put down as 'sis ke che'. Then I took a leaf and laid it under the page of my exercise book and rubbed over it with a green pencil. Atanasio watched as the outline and the veins began to appear right up to the curling elongated point. It looked so beautiful isolated on the white page and he looked approvingly at this record of his knowledge.

We moved on, the forest as thick and dense as I had wished for, the undergrowth as high as my head, the bigger trees rising into a green canopy, their straight smooth grey trunks with fluted buttresses to hold them on their way skyward, like enormous rockets. When the ceiba tree reaches the warmth of the sky, it spreads out its branches in a graceful umbrella. The Lacandon call it the 'god tree', and believe the Earth Lord, Kisin, lives among its roots waiting for the souls of the dead.

Atanasio slashed out our path with his machete, and I stopped looking out for nauyaca as I knew any sensible jumping pit viper, the nauyaca's family name, would have fled. As we walked, I tried to keep a sample leaf of each plant tucked among the pages of my notebook, some so big and rounded they flopped over the edges like green fabric.

'Mumu,' said Atanasio, and I recognised this one from the

compost workshop in San Cristobal, and remembered it was good for head lice. Head lice, internal parasites, upset stomachs, so far, except for snake bite, we were seeing all the maternal preoccupations of my post war childhood, when my sister and I were examined top and tail for evidence of any kind of infestation. Except that our heads were cleansed with paraffin, our guts dosed with bitter chocolate drops.

'Steep in hot water and then soak your hair with the lotion for 15 minutes, it kills the lice but you have to use it again two weeks later.'

Atanasio had become an enthusiastic mentor now, the act of passing on his knowledge gave him an animation that was such a contrast to his earlier mood. It was rare for him to talk about plant medicine with anyone, he said, and his son, grown up and married, was not interested in learning about forest plants.

'Although I tell him it is useful to know these cures, no, he doesn't want to look, to learn anything. There's not many of us left who know about plants.'

Even his wife used to be sceptical so when Atanasio described these leaves of *meke whech* and *nu kuch whech che* that together made a lotion to wash new babies, I wondered if his son was bathed on the first day of life with water strained from leaves his father gathered. And was it *pa pa che*, good for birth pangs and wombs, that convinced his wife that the old green cures work? I wasn't keeping up, my notes and leaf rubbings weren't always correlated. His wife's conversion came later, after the babies were grown.

'She had stomach pains and was becoming very weak,' he continued, 'but I prepared remedies for her and this restored her to health and strength.'

He moved from plant to plant, turning a leaf or scraping a piece of bark, me sweating and breathing hard behind him. We still moved uphill but I recovered when we stopped every few yards to examine more carefully certain roots, bark, leaves. Here was *hierba martinez* for earache and *hierba de tigre* for head and shoulder pains and yet more remedies for snake bite. The root of the female plant is stronger and more effective, I learnt, or I could use the leaves of another, male, plant, identified as such by its spines. Atanasio wrapped chips of wood in a leaf and secured it with a twist of vine, I tucked it in my shoulder bag. It's for mouth ulcers.

No amount of knowledge can prevent or halt every ailment, and so our talk moved on from the plants and their properties to people and their health and I discovered that epileptic Juanito is his brother. Everyone must be related in such a small community but it was surely another despondent twist that the last man who cared about plants and used them had a brother he couldn't help.

I stopped by a clump of orchids the colour of thick cream, they lay flowers up on a rotten lump of wood and I called to Atanasio to wait while I took a photograph. He watched, turned towards me and the camera, and I asked if I could take one of him and he stood there for another moment. I love to look at photographs, but not the intrusive act of taking them. It felt so awkward putting a camera between me and what I was part of a moment ago.

Later when I had the print I was very glad I followed my heart. Atanasio looks straight at me, serious and calm. And, unusually for me, the picture is in focus. Back in England I look at this photograph and see a thoughtful man who holds to his own unfashionable values while the people around him are changing.

The photo orchids didn't come out so well. The real ones looked so good against the jumble of green leaves. The white petals and sepals had a waxy texture but appeared as a fuzzy haze. There were so many orchids around us, attached to bark and rotting trunks, clustered on the lower branches and in the crooks of trees, anywhere they could cling and draw in food from the damp air. So many that some fell to settle on the forest floor into a litter made from leaves and ferns and a thousand broken branches, all decomposing into a perfect orchid nest. I tested one for fragrance, inhaling gently.

In the deep forest every level is a different world; at our feet, at eye level, above our heads and then away up in the canopy where the tallest trunks at last turn into branches. It is here in the canopy that the majority of forest creatures live, monkeys, birds, small cats, snakes. After my bold attempt at a photographic record, we carried on noticing things at ground level, a group of orchids sprouting from a piece of bark that had detached itself at some time. It was a new type for me, had tiny pink red blooms on the end of the thinnest of stems, and I wanted to take it for Tito's collection.

Tito had official approval to collect, and his zeal made him a champion for orchid survival. Wild orchids can't survive without the forest nor without people who have a passion for them. So I convinced myself that it was alright to take and placed it in my bag. But I felt similar doubts to when I took the photograph, divided between pure experience and that wanting to possess the experience. And I wanted to return something to Tito, who had given to me so generously. My doubt moved between taking as a regrettable habit or a survival instinct.

As we carried on with eyes to the ground Atanasio pointed out the scattered acorn husks, the remains of tropical sized acorns, 'Tepescuintle,' he said, 'pity I didn't bring my arrows, sometimes they're better than guns.' I was surprised to hear this, thinking the arrows were just a decorative home industry for selling in the markets. He smiled, 'Arrows are quiet.'

The only tepescuintle I'd seen was in an enclosure near the waterfall of Misol ha on the way to Palenque. The tepescuintle is a spotted pig like creature about two feet long, a big rodent and normally nocturnal. The ones whose dinner remains we were looking at must be fast asleep in burrows under the leaf mould.

'A year ago I killed two big ones and carried them down the hill. That was hard work, to carry them and use the machete, It's good coming out today, I get a path cleared.' Flora and now fauna had completed Atanasio's survey of his world.

Of course, I thought, Naha was like Lacanha, where each family had an area where they alone bathed, hunted, gathered and cultivated forest gardens. It was a sensible respect so one man didn't go crashing about disturbing or mistakenly shooting a neighbour. Just as in the English countryside, strangers and governments tend to think rainforest is a wilderness open to anyone.

I looked around and had no sense of where we were or how far we had come. I could tell only that where the ground sloped, it must lead down towards the road and the lake. We had set off soon after eight that morning and I couldn't see the sky or feel how hot the sun was, so had no idea how many hours we had been walking. Our discoveries took us uphill and sometimes along, Atanasio slashing a path through the thinnest growth.

If I turned to see our trail, I couldn't tell where we came from, branches had closed over the cut growth. It was at least mid day as the bird sounds of the cool morning had stopped. Sometimes I heard the shrilling of the insect that grows louder and louder then fades, like the passing of a high speed train. But as we reached a clearing, I looked up and saw a large bird outlined against the sky. I couldn't tell the colours but made out a small crested head. It stood upright and long legged on a high branch like a weathercock on a church spire.

'A pava,' said Atanasio following my look, pava which means peacock, and I felt proud of noticing it, even imagined he might be a tiny bit impressed.

When I checked my wildlife book days later I couldn't decide if it resembled the illustration of a great currasow, faisan real or a crested guan, pava cojolita. The latter was the name Atanasio had said. Spanish provided only an approximate translation of Mayan words, including names but then the bird was in the forest canopy, just as the book said and faison real, – the royal pheasant – is one which strolls about on the ground.

We arrived at Atanasio's regular track which wound down steeply and he advised me to turn sideways as I descended. Standing on the road again, he made sure I understood his message to Doña Bety, asking me to repeat it.

'Atanasio says hello and he and his family will come to visit later, at sunset.'

I felt stunned by emerging from shade into bright light, to me it was forest withdrawal symptoms. He waited for me to recover myself and added that if I wanted to go into the forest again, that was fine, and we could see more plants.

Visitors filled the camp all afternoon, and for a break, I walked up to the shop with Koh Maria, one of Chan Kin Viejo's two widows and after showing me to a small wood kiosk attached to someone's house, she continued to her family home. On the way back I called in to Juanito's cabin and asked about buying a set of bow and arrows; I have a friend in England whose surname is Fletcher. A set of arrows would make a perfect present.

At dusk, Atanasio arrived to see Doña Bety, with wife, son and daughter in law. His son ressembled him, taller than most of the Lacandon men, strong features, calm expression. The daughter in law was also tall compared to most women here, and robust looking. Perhaps she was a local Tzeltal girl; marrying in was encouraged. There were about 130 individuals in Naha, and therefore close relationships, resulting in the disposition for albinos, and maybe epilepsy. I met several men with Tzeltal wives and they were all bigger and fatter than the small, slight Lacandon girls. Tzeltal girls were farmers' daughters rather than forest gardeners and gatherers.

Juanito brought the bow and arrows that evening, accompanied by Don Antonio. I got a lesson in identifying the different arrowheads, clay, stone or wood, matching the prey for which they were shaped; otter, deer, wild turkey. Other black haired men in white tunics sat round the long table. Mountain village people, in particular those from Chamula, used to regard the 'longhairs' with alarm, and here in Naha, excepting for Atanasio, they were expressive and ready to joke and laugh and tease. I could see them enjoying their reputation as the evening became a men's night, lots of reminiscences and laughter about wild youth and tipsy ceremonies in the god house.

'But you don't do that anymore, do you,' said Fabiola.

'Yes, we do. Sometimes.' Chan Kin Cuarto replied, 'Antonio still calls us sometimes with the conch shell and we drink balché together. Not so many of us, but we do.'

Balché sounds delicious, a honey fermented drink made from the crushed bark of a tree belonging to the legume family. But it was a men only tipple reserved for rituals. While they talked, I was practising with my new toy, a little cut out gourd with a bark string. I was trying to make it spin like Juanito did. When I got the flick right, it hummed away on the table top and then everyone wanted to have a go. Above the noise, Antonio explained the best way to hold it and how to whip the string away cleanly, and then demonstrated. But it was still a lucky chance when I made it work.

Late in the night, Fabiola, Ian, Doña Bety and I sat silent after our social marathon. Then Ian and Fabiola, the married couple, went to their tent and Doña Bety and I, two grandmothers, remained companionably quiet while the fire died. We had become allies after the awkward start so many months ago. There was a curious information gap at Na Bolom. A black hole where what some people knew disappeared before it reached others. A common effect in any group, I imagine. At Na Bolom staff became unexpectedly redundant not needed from one day to the next. Like Auracelie crying behind her reception desk one day and gone the next. New staff appeared, without introduction, like Marisol and her boyfriend. I realised that no one had mentioned my arrival at Na Bolom's garden or why I was there.

I appreciated how every time Elisa, young and lively, acted as chaperone and cook for visits to the Lacandon it excluded Doña Bety. Doña Bety's long bond with people here at Naha and at Lacanha was passed over without anything being said. Now I understood her responses to me, and her unwelcoming attitude. I became Elisa's friend, accompanied her, and therefore contributed to Doña Bety's involuntary retirement. I was glad things had changed and I was no longer a usurper. We were friends.

But this reflective moment wasn't the end of the evening. Bor's elder brothers appeared, Chan Kin and Kayum, gliding into the clearing on a bike, one steering, one sidesaddle and carrying a guitar. The heavenly twins, as I thought of them, were rosier than Bor, with reddened cheeks and gold hair. And they weren't twins but close enough in age, 18 and 20, and looks, to be the twins of Popol Vuh, the Mayan creation story. These three sons of Chan Kin Cuarto bore, like their father did, the traditional names denoting their place in the family. Chan Kin, little sun, is the name of every eldest son, Kayum, lord of song, the second son, and Bor, third son and named for the bee. Three of the essential elements of life.

Chan Kin and Kayum weren't at all dismayed to find only the two of us and it wasn't long before Kayum clasped the guitar and sang a song of his own creation. He had a sweet low voice, the camp was still after the noisy excitement of the day and evening, and the forest became a silent presence. At that moment he was the spirit of his name, Kayum, lord of song. Then Chan Kin took the guitar, but he was hesitant, less tuneful and his brother prompted him occasionally, like his other half.

Their songs were about the old gods, but they learnt guitar by listening to music on a solar powered radio, and they had plans to go to a guitar class for the first time. It was probably in Tumbo, the biggest village in the area and which had a secondary school. This was a determined step as Tumbo is not a Lacandon but a Tzeltal settlement. 'Those who destroy the forest' as I heard a man from Naha say so scornfully. The brothers' songs were in Maya but they wanted to know about modern things, and had questions about the internet and email.

They also asked about Manon, a French Canadian student who stayed here for a few months researching her thesis. I remembered meeting her in the library at Na Bolom, and her saying, 'In Naha flirting is a glance, what seems polite curiosity to us carries much more.' In spite of this tentative enquiry from the heavenly twins, I recognised the emotion. How easy it is to love the stranger, they carry the world with them.

When the bike and guitar disappeared through the trees, Doña Bety did a final tidy up and I went off to the hut in the far corner for a pre sleep pee. As I sat down something bit my legs, a sharp warning bite, and I jumped up yelling and shone the torch to see hundreds of soldier ants and laughed with relief. Doña Bety, my saviour, rushed over with a pan of hot ashes and dumped them on the massed ranks marching through our long drop toilet hut. They climbed the wooden seat, a wide black line moving purposefully, and anything in their path, me, must be bitten out of the way.

Rolled into my hammock, the air chilled, the downpour began, and I slept to the roar of rain.

CHAPTER 15

Beneath The Earth's Surface

Composting in Na Bolom's garden hadn't changed a bit since the neighbourhood workshop in the church hall. The heaps remained scattered with pine needles and scraps of plastic, street dogs pawed over kitchen waste and grackles uttered harsh cries from pinnacles of mixed debris. It was the lack of manure that daunted me, I told myself. With manure, I could attempt to layer these hillocks and shape them into steaming hot order.

Manvel, content with the respect he received at the workshop, carried on the same as always in his vegetable area up by the laundry line, every so often strewing the beds with compost complete with glass, plastic and pine needles. The carrots and spinach continued to cope magnificently, but I craved to tuck them in with a rich dark cover, compost cooked to perfection with a wholesome nourishing aroma.

A visit to La Albarrada, the horticultural place, was always in the back of my mind since learning that Antonio worked there. That was the answer, there would be manure there. So I took a bus to the outskirts of town where homebuilt houses sprouted erratically between patches of maize and vegetables, shops and mechanics' workshops. It was a direction I'd never been to before, Maria Auxiliadora.

The bus was a dented white one, one up in size from a minibus with plenty of standing room. A boy hung off the step and called out the sing song syllables. *Ma ri a* given three long syllables and then *Auxiliadora* in one breath. His job was also to warn the driver to stop or start, hustle passengers on, and give change from a stack of pesetas held in one curled hand. When we arrived at my nearest stop, the bus driver pointed the way along a dirt road.

La Albarrada is my ideal, the one I aspire to and never achieve, rows of neatly weeded plants, clusters of flowers, stands of saplings, and clipped hedges. The sun shone and wooden shingled roofs glowed merging into the mountains behind. I imagined Manvel's voice intoning, 'organic, everything is organic, organic is good,' as I signed in at the entry post and walked alongside a privet hedge out of which rose a life size topiary woman and a sheep almost as large as its shepherdess.

Where paths crossed, wooden signs pointed the way to a wormery, herbarium, print and weaving workshops, even women's hostels, men's hostels and a creche. I stopped to find a human being in this utopian scene and get some guidance on manure. Even the main office looked organic, as if it had grown slowly out of the earth, a low but spacious cabin, made of logs with a wooden floor, plants dappled the inside of large windows.

Hearing my accent the director came out to inspect me. She was young and serious, and intrigued to welcome a foreign visitor,

'You must look at everything and please talk to the students, they come from poor villages all over Chiapas and so most of our courses are residential. Everything is provided free. La Albarrada's job is to raise standards and help people to earn more. One person can influence their whole community with their new skills and optimism.'

Her words sounded practical and enthusiastic. The idea of one person as a catalyst for changing their world appealed, why was it that I struggled to change one bit of mine. She laughed when I asked about manure. I must have been one of the few people in San Cristobal without animals somewhere in the extended family. Even my fellow participants in the compost workshop had chickens, or hamsters. She said, 'There are no animals here at La Albarrada, no manure.'

Maybe I could ask the workshop tutors where to find manure but

I already decided it would be easier to tuck a shovel under my jacket and wait for the firewood carrying mule I saw in Calle Tapachula. Micaela Cruz Perez directed me to the wormery, the phone rang and she went to answer it, calling back, 'and there's a theatre performance at 4pm. In the hall.'

I thought I was coming to a horticultural training place and the further I walked the more I saw a cross fertilisation of materials. Scraps of leather amd metal became a large sculpture of a horse and rider poised over the landscape, plastic bottles became holders for tree seedlings, tree trunks made play structures, and hedges sprouted clipped stars and sheep, as if arriving here set off a burst of playful inventiveness.

A group of young men chatted in Tzotzil or maybe it was Tzeltal or Chol, whichever it was, they were descended from one of the Mayan city states the Spanish encountered. And very likely they were performing the same trades, weaving and leather work and growing much the same food as their ancestors, above all maize. These young men tested their strength on the wooden bars doing pull ups and turns on the rings of the outdoor gym, laughing at each other before going off to one of the workshop buildings.

All the buildings were one storey wooden cabins with pine shingle roofs, some extended by fitting several hexagonal or octagonal cabins together. Marimba music came out of somewhere, and I wound my way through raised beds of carrots and aubergines until I got to a different sort of building, a block shed with tin roof. This was the wormery.

It was hot inside, black plastic insulated the roof and a bright naked bulb illuminated several pens of vegetable matter. A small man in a straw cowboy hat mashed up maize cobs in a tub. He paused and leant on his stick to talk to a semi circle of men also in cowboy hats who soon turned to stare at me. I remembered the poster in the main office 'all women are free and equal' but presumably women didn't exercise their freedom to choose worm breeding.

'I work in the garden at Na Bolom,' I said to explain my presence, 'and I've heard a lot about La Albarrada and wanted to see the wormery.'

Meliton Perez Perez introduced me to the red californian worms breaking down the remains of maize cobs and his students crowded round pointing out the different stages. 'We start with fifty worms and they multiply with so much food and then we have rich stuff to put on our fields,' said one keen student. Maestro Meliton added, 'it must be californian worms, not just any earthworms.'

The men were delighted to take me on a short guided tour of the shed. I admired the thin wine red worms, a multitude of veins criss crossing the yellowy white maize pulp, then peered into the tubs of soaking cobs, while everyone displayed their knowledge in chorus. 'They have to soak in water for twelve hours.' they repeated. 'And they must be well mashed.'

I didn't think of asking where these cobs came from, probably a maize processing plant. I imagined these were the residue of all the cobs, bought every evening in the plaza, steamed in pots or grilled on charcoal in front of the maize yellow cathedral walls, their fat yellow grains, 'our lord's sunbeams and precious gift,' nourishing the people. Here was their ultimate use, the cores transformed by industrious worms, red the colour of the east and renewal, ready to be returned to the earth.

I left the farmers and followed the worm master's suggestion to look at the herbarium next. A young woman hanging screen prints up to dry caught my attention and I hesitated to look through the open glass doors. A turtle swam on the page and I wondered why the image of a turtle, here, so far from the sea. Like most of the women I passed on the grassy paths Angela wore clothes that identified her home and it too was a long way from the coast. The flowery flounce on her blouse announced Oxchuc, a Tzeltal village so I knew that must be her first language, one of the at least thirty forms of Mayan. Spanish was her second, as it was mine.

My La Albarrada day became a confirmation of that language epiphany, the epiphany that happened in the compost workshop. Now I was swimming, metaphorically speaking, at one with the surroundings, more or less gracefully. And definitely afloat. A turtle could be my emblem, apparently awkward but a steady swimmer.

'Why a turtle?' I asked.

'So I can sell tee shirts.' she answered cryptically. 'In Ocosingo market. I'll put a different creature on other tee shirts, so when people go home they remember the ones that live in Chiapas. You didn't know they are endangered? You see, you do now,' she laughed.

Angela was twenty years old, a confident wage earner, an artisan selling embroidered blouses, like so many others, but she wanted to learn new skills. The other women were busy with the tutor and their designs. She had the optimism that the Micaela Cruz Perez spoke of, how could she fail to inspire others in the market at Ocosingo. They would surely want to know where she got that from. Angela walked me to the herbarium and introduced me to Antonia, who sat at a table spread with dried leaves, La Albarrada's resident herbalist. Her work might be traditional but she was a town dweller dressed in modern clothes. We sat round her table while she put herbs into envelopes and talked to us.

'My mother is a midwife and I saw how she worked, how women relied on her. There aren't many doctors in rural places. She knew so much about plants and as I grew up that was part of my life. So I studied to be a herbalist out of an interest that was always there.'

I told her that I bought lemon grass bundles, long coarse strips folded and tied, sold in the market and from street stalls, made tea from a few strands steeped in hot water and simmered until the grass turned yellowy green and the scent of lemon perfumed my kitchen. There were dried plants for sale that I hadn't tried, all with some recommendation for ailments, and some I had. My love of black tea, English pots of tea at intervals all through the day and evening, was suspended. I forgot my intake of caffeine and tannin instead tea in Chiapas meant camomile or lemongrass or hibiscus.

Antonia explained that lemongrass stimulates the digestive juices and was an appetite improver, that it calmed indigestion, especially that caused by over use of hot spices or alcohol. I felt extraordinarily healthy after hearing that, since I suffered none of the latter. My digestion was a marvel of appreciation, use of hot spices and alcohol modest. She showed me plants for skin problems and plants for headaches and plants for every possible disease.

'This is for TB, and you use the whole plant to make a tea to drink every day. The students here learn the importance of a botanic garden, how to grow these plants and where to grow each one. And they learn how to prepare pomades and lotions. Have you been to the Mayan medicine herbarium?'

I had and disappointed the herbalist there with my lack of illness. Antonia gave me advice on plants to augment the medicine plot at Na Bolom. But what was most fascinating was how many of her students were conventional doctors and nurses.

'Doctors want to understand what their patients believe in, they want to learn about the characteristics of healing plants.'

And what better teacher could they have than Antonia Hernandez Ortiz, daughter of a rural midwife who grew up to study what she saw and absorbed around her. The division between the ancient mix of ritual and plants and modern rational treatment was closing and at times the two approaches blend.

Even in town homes herbal remedies were common, as I found when talking to the school children on their visit to Na Bolom's garden, and the pharmacies sold commercially prepared versions. Traditional healers, curanderas, like the young bird guide Javier's grandmother and the shamans I saw in the church at Chamula rolling eggs over the body of their patients, they didn't need a course like this. Like Antonia they grew up with herbal medicine.

In the forest, source of thousands of plants, many with undiscovered properties, that knowledge, according to Atanasio was set aside in the desire to know new ways. The cycle of acquiring knowledge that is under our noses, quite literally, abandoning it for modernisation and then the rediscovering like Antonia's conventionally trained doctor students, was happening here on the edge of a town.

Angela with her plaited hair around her brow, regional dress and enterprising personality and Antonia in plaid skirt and jumper, quiet and serious, said together.

'Nearly four o'clock, she must see the play.' And one on each side they guided me along to the hall.

It was long past starting time and the audience still filtered into the hall and nothing appeared on stage. Children sat on the floor at the front playing, some looking happily at the empty stage. In front of me sat all the mothers and older sisters, whose shiny black plaits tied with satin ribbons flicked to and fro accompanying animated conversations.

Antonia introduced me to her friend, 'Maria is a midwife like my mother.'

We shook hands and I asked what the play was about.

'My work, that's what it's about. It's called Viva la Vida,' said Maria. 'You'll see everything I do and everything I have to deal with, like the husbands.'

Maria seemed capable of dealing with anything. I did find out that the play was about maternal mortality, higher than it should be, in the remote country places that La Albarrada was here to serve. Everyone seemed very cheerful and enthusiastic at the prospect of an hour on the subject. There was a first night buzz about the audience. Men arrived too, and stood around at the back or leant against the walls as if they might be held responsible and need a quick getaway. Then a woman's voice began to sing offstage and the hall went quiet.

She sang a lament. The spotlight focused on a dying woman, her young daughter placing candles by her feet and head. Death crossed the stage in a skeleton costume, and the ghost of the woman rose to follow but paused to warn her daughter to know better.

All the parts in this company were played by women. Men? Easy, add boots and a swagger, a lick of hair showing under a cowboy hat. Scenes moved through courtship and marriage, with love transforming into familiar and predictable roles for men and women; the bar for men and the kitchen for women, male authority and female obedience. But this time the heroine remembered she had a promise to fulfill. She must, as in all the best stories, do what she believed in undeterred by others, even the king of her heart.

The memory of her mother's fate stayed with her, and her husband, the laugh winning lovable rogue, was won over by her strength of character. He took his wife to have regular check ups at the clinic and the local midwife delivered a heathy child.

As the heroine and her baby slept, the mother appeared in her dream. 'Viva la vida!' she murmured. We sat in a haze of sadness, laughter and happy fulfillment, and clapped like mad. A happy ending on stage but as I mixed with people afterwards I met a girl who told me that this was her story too.

'My mother died when she had my brother. I was eleven years old.'

Matter of fact words but also a little island of remembered loss among the women and children chatting around her. She was sixteen and didn't plan to marry for a long time. Her younger siblings needed her.

Fomma, Fortaleza de la Mujer Maya, meaning 'the strength of the Mayan woman', has been going for a few years. The five women, from two Mayan communities, created issue based plays with help from a professional theatre director, Doris Difarnecio. They played villages and towns, for schools and any group who needed them. Doris offered me a lift in their white minibus, sitting with five women from twenty something to fifties, short and solid, round faces pleased with another well received performance.

They waved goodbye to La Albarrada like princesses with their long hair or crown of plaits, dressed in ankle length skirts, handwoven wool or blue jean, stitched satin blouses or cardigans. 'Here, here's our other programme,' and Petrona gave me a flyer for 'The Right to Vote'.

Local elections were coming up and already posters proliferated on telephone poles and walls; photos of men, each bordered with party colours, green and red for PRI and blue for PAN and green for the PRD. I knew Manvel was an unshakeable PRI man, because I asked him what he thought about the parties and he said Chamula was always PRI.

After an astonishing seventy years in power, since the Mexican Revolution, whose heroes named so many streets in San Cristobal, PRI was finally ousted and PAN voted in. That was a national election. Local elections had their particular loyalties. Patricio, fluent in Tzotzil filled me in with the historical agenda, such as how the local PRI man was reputed to be the one responsible for the Acteal massacre in 1997, the powerful shadow behind the paramilitary assassins.

I wondered what the new play included. 'It's all from improvisation, not a proper rehearsed theatre play like we do with Doris, we're doing this in the plaza and anywhere we can,' Petrona informed me.

Doris added, 'Most of our plays start with stories then I help to shape it. That's my role. But what did you think of the dead mother's appearance? We wanted her to move differently, lightly like a spirit. She wasn't too bouncy?'

'Not too bouncy at all.' I said, 'everyone loved it.'

Robert Laughlin and I sat on a sofa in front of a wood fire. The room was long and plain, white lime washed walls, tall dark wood doors opening to a garden where, he said, the humming bird moth came to the tiger lilies at dusk. We had been looking at his book, Metaphors of the Heart. Each metaphor was illustrated on the opposite page. This was the new book, if any of Bob's books could be called new, they spent so long in gestation. This one spent maybe ten years in the making, not as many years as others. The Great Tzotzil Dictionary took fourteen.

The drawings for Metaphors of the Heart were rediscovered by chance one night. Wandering about the house during a bout of insomnia, he pulled out a drawer and found the lost folder. Before the final step of becoming a book in a bookshop, the manuscript was dismissed by one publisher, 'as about as interesting as a sheep.' Not the right thing to say to a man who had spent most of his adult life among people for whom the sheep is a holy symbol, a beloved and sacred animal.

I sat here in this sparse, old house with a man I admired through his thirty years work. An anthropologist, Robert Laughlin studied and immersed himself in the important aspects of life, plants, language, saints, devils, of a particular part of the Chiapas highlands. I came to know the Mayan world better because I read People of the Bat, his collection of dreams and tales from Zinacantan, one of the two influential and distinctive parishes in the nearest mountains to San Cristobal. Zinacantan, the parish I still thought of as the pink parish because when I first visited there ten years ago that was the predominant colour. Pink, a stinging bright pink.

The residents of Zinacantan had dreams that resembled Chagall's paintings. They appeared lighthearted, frivolous, not fully attached to a mundane world and often spiting adversity through wilful foolishness. Reading the dreams I burst out laughing or envied their energy, as Zinacantecans walked and fought and dug and planted as busily as in daily life. Then there was the relentless chattiness of these sleep states. All the participants of each dream; friends, enemies, devils and domestic animals, had conversations with the dreamers, 'a numinous realm of souls, all of whom act as agents in the theatre of the dream.'

Some slumbering part of me was charged up by the remarkable sleep adventures of Romin and Anselmo and other men, and women, a night world transcribed by Bob Laughlin. Bob had the imagination to record the dreams just as they were, and became a hero for me. He understood those things, as the Mayans say, 'beyond the earth's surface,' and took the trouble to remind others how valuable they are, these dream messages, metaphors.

Each page of Metaphors of The Heart showed a phrase translated from the Tzotzil, recorded by a Spanish monk in colonial times. The illustrations and text were printed onto handmade paper, paper made from flowers and palm leaves and maize tassels. Maybe some that grew from Na Bolom's garden. Two women had come to pick bags full of plant material to soak and press and turn into paper and I helped them to collect up overblown pink crinum lily blossoms that had fallen onto the paths. Thick and waxy enough to almost make paper on their own, the blatant trumpets acquired a subtlety as paper for heart metaphors.

The heart is knowledge
The heart is a warrior

Before I left I wanted to know what happened to Romin and Anselmo who taught Bob so much, so cheerfully. 'Romin just turned yellow one day and died. He did drink a lot of pox. Pox opens the mind to the world of the saints but the liver wasn't up to it, not the amount Romin absorbed.'

'And what about you?' I asked, 'Did listening to their dreams make you remember yours? Did you begin to have powerful dreams of your own.'

At the time of reading People of The Bat, I thought that if I drew in inspiration and felt in touch with some part of my mind I usually ignored, what about the recorder, the man who listened and wrote down these dreams. Did he reflect on his own sleep visitors. Was it catching this dreaming, I asked. This was the dream he told me, Bob's dream.

'I was staying at Na Bolom, in Frans Blom's old room. It wasn't so easy to get to the villages before everyone had trucks. San Cristobal was quiet then, smaller and contained, Na Bolom was a house set between the town and a ranch, grass and cattle all around and a few farmhouses nearby. I used to go back there and write up my notes, take a break from staying at the house in Zinacantan Centre. It was there I dreamt of a shaman who tried to kill me.

He was a neighbour who when drunk was a vengeful, demanding brujo if refused a drink, and it wasn't acceptable in Zinacantan society to go around asking for drink. In the dream he faced me holding an axe, I saw him rushing towards me becoming smaller and smaller until he disappeared into my forehead. I felt the blow.

The next day I went back to Zinacantan and the shaman's old wife and his sister came immediately and warned me about this man saying that the previous evening he had taken an axe and was looking out to get me.

If someone steps outside the social rules, he is a lost person, and this man because he was a shaman became a dangerous lost person, a threat to the whole community. Some time later his body was found on the sacred mountain, he had been castrated.'

The power of dreams works away and brings insights at unforeseen moments. On the surface of the dream, Bob was in danger from the shaman, a real and unpredictable person, but you can't collect the contents of others' dreams and remain with a mind closed off from your own. I didn't ask Bob for any explanation or meaning. What he saw was for him. Just to listen brought thoughts useful for my own self. I saw the shaman dream as a classic of having your mind opened, cutting straight through the bonehead. A warning and an alarm call from the gods whether to an anthropologist or to me, this listener, of dangers on any path to wisdom and a test of courage and steadfastness.

Illumination implies a sudden understanding, and a terrifying experience like Bob's ensures it will never be forgotten. Perhaps that's why I was drawn back to Mayan Mexico after so many years. My meeting with Pablo Canche on the beach at Tulum, the hurricane that followed and the terror and the danger of that moment 'fixed' Chiapas and the Mayan world in my mind.

Since I read People of the Bat, I wanted a dream of my own, I wanted to see 'beneath the earth's surface', not merely know of it. A dream would affirm my efforts at a real understanding of all I met in Chiapas, but no dream appeared until one evening at a meditation session I had a glimpse of the other world.

Carolina, the scornful, the materialist, was an unlikely believer in meditation so her enthusiasm convinced me to accompany her to the centre in the lower hills above the town. We walked through the gates and past an old house on two floors, a balcony running across the first floor, the remains of a country house or ranch but not yet, like my house, completely surrounded by newer building. The owner's riding horses grazed around us, flicking their tails and dancing away if we came too near. The meditation centre was on the next plot of land and in the dusk the town began to light up and in the mountains a few sparkles appeared.

The dynamic meditation appealed to me more than just sitting. Each week the movement was different, and this week it was a salute to the four corners of the world. We threw an arm forward as if in the grand gesture of a Spanish courtier, then made a three quarters turn, repeating this at each of the four directions. A continuous whirling dervish movement but forward and back, low and high, graceful and rhythmic. After this we sat, eyes closed and the teacher asked us to visualise. So hard to stop doing and just allow my mind to accept what comes, good when I do.

Untranslatable, unexplainable to myself, the images arrived, not dreams, nor challenging events, no conversations with people, animals or gods. A great lake appeared ringed with pine trees, a canoe drawn up before me, mountains opposite. Still, silent, immense. The image asked nothing of me, no action, it was there, available; rock, water, trees. Energy radiated from my body.

This happened after I read People of the Bat and before I met Bob Laughlin. My experience in the meditation reminded me to find out if he too had found himself affected by those dreams. Bob wasn't the kind of anthropologist who was rigidly academic, he was friendly, engaged, with a sense of humour as wicked and ridiculous as any of his informants. I was glad to hear he also dreamt. Perhaps the spooks and the Earth Lord wanted to shake him up a little, tease him at the very least. One way of being acknowledged by those dark powers.

The girls who love Elisa sat on the steps with handfuls of woven bracelets, the grumpy ice cream seller who was also a fan of Elisa ignored potential customers and leant against his hand cart to look at a group of women with a banner. I went closer to see what was happening and the girls ran over, hung on my arms and asked about their friend, 'Elisa? Elisa? When is she coming back to San Cristobal?'

'She called me and said tell the children she is in the city taking photos and she will come and show you the pictures soon,' I answered. I wanted this to be true. Happy, we all joined the circle around the women and their banner and I saw it was a performance of The Right To Vote.

Petrona sat on a chair being a typical housewife, while her neighbour challenged her to think why she voted and for whom. Every face in the circle stared at Petrona, as if to see her thoughts as she listened. The neighbour set out the ideal for a woman with a mind of her own, and Petrona's traditional character resisted. The argument was elaborated, objections considered and vanquished, until an agreement was reached that women could, and must, think for themselves. The male character, Rosita in a mask and hat, a know it all lord of the house appeared and dismissed any women's equality nonsense. He made everyone laugh but this was no pantomime.

The scenario unfolded to show what everyone knew; that there were regional loyalties, just as there were in my own country, and those loyalties secured practical rewards; grants, influence and permits. More than that, if the man of the family voted PRI or PAN, then so did the women. And if one parish had divided party allegiances then that often caused violence.

At the beginning of Lent, that intense time before the celebration of Easter and the renewal of hope, a clash over government money, between adherents of the two main parties, ended with the death of a boy of seventeen. He died from loss of blood, the mark of Ash Wednesday still on his forehead because political opponents stopped the ambulance from reaching him. So I understood the risks if women made their own choice.

The circle was almost all Mayan, country people, and those who lived in the poor outskirts of the town, used to politicians as the devil you know is better than the one you don't. The play cut through that acceptance. The girls and young women traders stopped selling, turned their backs on the cathedral plaza and stood there gripped by a drama they knew well. The shoeshine boys left their posts and sat on their footstools chin in hands watching and listening to the essential matters of choice set out by a few stout women dressed like their mothers in embroidered blouses and aprons. As they say in Tzotzil, 'Mi stak?' Can we? and the answer was 'Stak!' We can!

Like the people at La Albarrada, who wanted a chance to find out how to ensure a just reward for their labours, the players and onlookers wanted to know that they had choice. A choice to draw inspiration from their dreams, subconscious and conscious, and the choice to bring them into being.

Sometimes at the evening meal there was a kind of discussion that excited and yet made me feel uneasy; talk about Mexico, its economy, its problems. It was the foreign and Mexico City visitors that initiated these and it woke me up from my subjective state, sharpened my thoughts. Other times the talk was about 'them', the indigenous, Tzotziles, Tzeltales, Lacandones, and 'it', the land and development.

One such evening I sat next to Delphine a French woman married to a Mexican and with whom she ran a restaurant near Palenque, the most visited archaeological site in Chiapas. When I asked her, a long time resident, for her inside view, she changed, sounded defensive and angry.

'They want to take over, the indigenous,' she said, 'They're not interested in working, you know, they just want to take. And there's so many.'

We slipped from French back into Spanish and the Lacandon man opposite, appearing to hear only the word Palenque, joined our conversation. A big handsome man, and blind. His long hair and tee shirt with Renegade in large letters, added to his striking presence. I had met him before, here and in Lacanha on the way to Kayum Maax and Chanakin's house. I admired how he used conversation to recompense for loss of sight. In seconds he charmed my companion, he even knew of her restaurant and before we finished coffee, had been invited to be her guest. When she left, the renegade man and I sat on.

'What a transformation. How did you do that?' I asked.

'Darkness can clarify the mind,' he replied.

CHAPTER 16

The Mouth of Heaven

I have a piece of shell from the beach at Boca del Cielo. It's flat and thick, imprinted on one side with a palm tree shape and four diagonal slits like sun rays, the other side with wavy seaweed fronds. These patterns are made of tiny pinpricks, holes for breathing or filtering the sea and arranged as if the shell, when occupied, was a living representation of land and sea.

Boca del Cielo, the name translates as the mouth of heaven or mouth of the sky, is a small fishing village where the river widens before it's swallowed up by the sea. It felt the right place to pause and relax as my going home to England date drew near. A few more weeks at Na Bolom and my work there would be finished. The coast was a new part of Chiapas for me, and I chose this place on the tropical lowland bounded by the Sierra Madre mountain chain and the Pacific. At Na Bolom I was always occupied and always thinking ahead to something else I wanted to know, like a dog who couldn't stop turning around before settling down to rest. This would be my holiday on the beach moment, my first moment away from anything or anyone to do with work at Na Bolom and even then it still had to be in Chiapas.

From San Cristobal the minibus took the zigzag road down to the plains and the state capital, Tuxtla. From Tuxtla I travelled by coach 300 kilometres through the Sierra Madre until the air became hotter and damper as we approached the Pacific. Men in cowboy hats with horseriders' beautiful upright backs joined the bus and talked about cattle. Grasslands became the new landscape and even the driver's radio changed stations, and tuned in to ranchero music, plaintive cowboy love songs.

At dusk I arrived in the last big town before Tapachula near the Guatemalan border, notorious for narcotraficante murders. The last local minibus had left. It was a taxi or stay the night. That's when I broke my Finsbury Park rule. If I won't do it in Finsbury Park, then I won't do it anywhere else in the world. I pondered this in a taxi with two men speeding through heavy rain along an unlit road towards a place I'd never been to. The driver picked his brother up along the way who then tried to flatter me.

'You are sixty? No. Maybe about fifty something. Perhaps you will meet a nice Chiapeneco husband.'

And he leant forward and stretched an arm along the back of my seat. I sat next to the driver, his face grim, eyes focussed on the waterfall drenching the windscreen. That's when I remembered the Finsbury Park rule. As usual there was nothing I could do. I had no idea where we were or how long it would take to Boca del Cielo, which for all I knew might have been washed away. I sat back and enjoyed the conversation. How my Spanish had improved.

My trust was rewarded when we arrived. The brothers insisted on finding me a place to stay, asking at two hotels closed after the summer crowds, before handing me over to one where the patron agreed to open. An hour later I was eating a spicy prawn broth on the terrace by an empty swimming pool. A thousand cicadas hummed in the background, a bass line to the parrot cries from an aviary across a garden of stocky palm trees. The evening air was heavy and still, the proprietors silent. I smoked a cigarette and even this was an effort.

Boca del Cielo curves round a lagoon, and I planned to stay at one of the restaurants on the strip of land between the lagoon and the ocean.

My journey for a place of rest wasn't complete yet. Bus, coach, taxi and now boat. I had a recommendation to a restaurant with a couple of beach huts. 'And the food is good.' The furthest and simplest shelter appealed, and closest to the nothingness of an ocean after the busy months in Na Bolom's garden.

The next morning I took a narrow wooden lancha to Doña Marta's place across the lagoon, motoring across brown water decorated with bright red patches like turkey rugs. I looked with dismay at this unappealing water.

'It won't stay, that red stuff,' the boatman reassured me. 'It's the storm, the water brings earth from the mountains and red from the mangrove leaves. Lucky the holiday people have gone.'

The strip was barely a hundred yards wide, and lined with open air cafes and restaurants facing the lagoon and the land. All the buildings, made of wood or bamboo with palm thatch roofs, were fronted by competing signs advertising the restaurants and their fishy menus. All were silent after the summer holidays, the families which a week ago crowded the tables had returned to towns. Visitors arrived by fishing boat and stepped into their chosen place. I stepped into Doña Marta's, but one guest didn't seem to disturb her. It was September and I appeared to have the place to myself.

She showed me a cabin in the dunes above the Pacific Ocean. In a few steps I became Robinson Crusoe. The beach was endless and empty. A burning blue sky and sea striped white with sand and breakers. I spent a week sleeping in an airy bamboo room, sitting in the sparse shade of the coconut palms, reading, eating lots of fish, watching pelicans and frigate birds diving and skimming the breakers. In the evenings I finished supper, leant my arms on the table and watched telenovelas from the television set on a high shelf.

From Marta's restaurant I looked across the lagoon and saw how small Boca del Cielo was among the intense green of trees and climbing plants. Behind the village, mountains dominated, not pointed volcanic guardians this time but the Sierra Madre, a flat topped range of stately yellow ridges. This was my breakfast view from one of the oil-cloth covered tables under the palm thatch roof.

Doña Marta had a husband, Francisco, and a fifteen year old daughter whose name I never found out. The daughter's equally young boyfriend kissed her while Marta made me coffee in the little kitchen. Each restaurant had at least one boat drawn up on to sandy mud or among tree roots, the men supplied the seafood ingredients and the women cooked. Francisco went out every late afternoon or early morning into the mangroves or joined other fishermen in a graceful group, the prows lifting like an eager flock of seabirds as they set out towards the open sea.

In the humid afternoons, I retired to a hammock like the family. Mine hung inside my cabin. I had a camp bed for nights and imagined Simon Bolívar, the champion of a pan Latin America, using one like this on military campaigns, a tall folding wooden frame and thick canvas. The hammock was for siestas, the open strings stopped sweat accumulating and I put my foot down on the sand floor to induce a gentle swing, while I dozed, watched lizards, read a book even.

The first day, I tried to swim in the lagoon when the water cleared of its red mangrove debris, but it was too shallow and only good for looking down at the shoals of tiddlers. So I went to the sea and I couldn't understand why it's called Pacific, the breakers knocked me down and dragged me under the surf, my haunch scraped raw before I found the strength to get upright. Each day I struggled into the water, part of my self imposed holiday, manoeuvred my way past the waves into the swell and swam. Even then I felt a pull of oceanic power and didn't stay long. It was the only demanding, and invigorating, moment of the day.

After a few days total leisure and unused to this somnolent life, I roused myself to walk to the end of the sandbar where the lagoon meets the sea. It didn't take long, my expedition, the spit soon narrowed and ended with shallow waves marking a line across from sand tip to the opposite curve of coast. It was when I turned to walk back that I noticed green army tents, low to the ground, and soldiers in camouflage, leaning against the tent poles with guns in their arms. The camp was full on to the hot salt wind, a tiny camp where the trees and land became sandy scrub.

That marked the end of my lazy, empty days. The next morning there was another swimmer, and when I staggered out of the waves and sat down, the figure walked towards me. She was young and bikinied, and staying at a cafe further along if I walked in the other direction, the walk next on my brief list of exertions. As we talked I picked out shells from among all the tiny bits of shore debris, small and yellow shells or pointed curly ones. A sea shell represented zero in the Mayan number system, and placed next to a number increased its value. A boat moved south between the beach and the horizon.

'Not a fishing boat,' I commented.

'If it was night I'd say on it's way to collect cocaine in Tapachula.' said Anna, 'Maybe it is anyway.'

I told her about the army post. It made sense now.

'There's lots of illegal boats along here, because it's so near the border. The army arrest some, ignore others. Maybe they do their own business too.'

At night I never walked the few steps through the trees to look out at the sea. The beach was my day place. I ate supper and watched Amor Real under the dim electric bulbs slung across the roof struts. I became addicted to this historical drama, its unbuttoned flounced shirts and babies of rich but uncertain parentage. Any dramas offshore I had not noticed. Anna filled me in with all the possibilities.

'A week ago they arrested an Italian. He was living here like a recluse for two years, had a little house, people liked him. They said he was wanted in Italy, that he was one of the Red Brigade, on the run for a long time.'

'We're leaving tomorrow.' she said, 'Come and have coffee with us. It's real coffee. They have an Italian coffee maker.'

Enticing. Marta made instant and I craved the hit of the rich Chiapaneco roast that I was used to. The hiss of the machine, the aroma, the conversation brought me to life even before I tasted the good coffee. A few days of silence ended. My salty skin glowed and I finger combed my tangled hair. I heard that Anna and her boyfriend were also at the big gathering in August at Oventik, the Zapatista civilian centre near San Cristobal. I listened to yet another version of what took place.

Everyone I knew who went, including myself, was unsure whether any of the EZLN comandantes were there or not and whether statements were made or not. Although one version made sense – that any talk took place early in the morning before the town supporters arrived. I thought again of Elisa, she would tell me yet another Zapatista story and that would be soon. Wherever she was we had agreed to meet before I left Mexico.

According to Anna this apparent, almost mischievous uncertainty wasn't intended at all. It wasn't, as so many saw it, part of the Marcos mystique, but was just a perception by those who were used to public agendas and timetables.

'There were speeches on the Friday night, and anyway it's not about comandantes and guerilleros anymore, it's about developing the local self government, isn't it?'

So I had another glimpse into the meaning of 'caracoles'. The change of emphasis from armed rebels to civilians; the caracoles.

Before the sun was high and impossibly hot, I said goodbye and continued along the beach. Alone again, I was the only human being in the world. The incline from beach to trees hid all signs of human activity, I saw only a natural world. I walked on and on until I reached the mangroves which clustered where fresh water met salt.

The beach became wilder with scrubby bushes and then I saw a net enclosure some way above the waterline, with rows of little markers like a toy cemetery. I stopped to examine the writing on the cross bars. Each cross had a written date. A breeze block building squatted behind, the only one on the long stretch of sand, but no one was visible through the window, and the door was padlocked.

I looked around and came across a well, except that it wasn't a well but a round pool with high sides and down in the water a full grown turtle wafted its front flippers. Mesmerised by this big gentle creature I sat on the parapet wondering if it noticed me and if I was any sort of interest to it. A metal plaque described this turtle as a golfina, *Lepidochelys olivacea.*

After a while I walked through to the lagoon side which I saw was the official entrance of the compound; a wooden sign said, Turtle Research Station. A large laminated poster showed every variety of turtle and I picked out the golfina. A lancha pulled up outside the sign and a couple got out and went into the building, I wandered by and said hello. They called me in and I asked about the strange rows of dated crosses.

'That's where we bury the turtle eggs. The date is so we know when they will hatch out. We collect the eggs to protect and monitor them. You know, some people like to eat them, for them, they are food, wild food.'

He showed me the day's hatchlings in a bucket, a mass of miniature turtles, all trying to climb out, already desperate to get to the sea. Each hatchling was the length of my thumb, would fit into the cup of my hand.

'We release them at dusk, then they have a better chance of survival. The birds swoop on them as they run to the water if they hatch where the eggs are laid.'

Fredy and Maria were biologists and husband and wife. They visited the research station by day and at night went out searching for newly laid eggs. I had always thought turtles laid their eggs at the same time, that there were a few days or even one night when every turtle arrived in a great egg laying event governed by the full moon or the tides. I imagined the dome of their shells rising out of the sea like a fleet of small submarines, then the steady clamber up the sand, a marathon dig and an orgy of egg deposit. Beaches do exist, just as I imagined, where turtles come ashore in such numbers that this has a special word, *arribadas*, the arrival. But on most beaches it is not such a dramatic group surge but a quieter, modest event.

'A few females come ashore most nights in July, August and September,' said Fredy. 'Come with us. Be here at eleven and wear trousers, it's cold on the bike.'

I left them checking the dates for the next batch of turtles. Happy that I had roused myself out of the patch of sand that was Marta's place, I walked back in the growing heat towards more fried fish for lunch.

In the Mexican cookery book I bought for my son, published in the 1970s and chosen above other cookery books for the stories surrounding the ingredients and recipes, there was a recipe for turtle soup. One recipe without a story perhaps because it would be unpalatable. Before official protection, the sea turtles, the golfina among them, were eaten towards extinction and their eggs plundered. Turtles were treated, as Fredy said, as free food, killed greedily, or mutilated by cutting off their flippers for leather and left to drown. Harvested to the point they became endangered.

Chances of survival have improved for the turtle, in Boca del Cielo it is Fredy and Maria who carry out the Cites agreement. CITES, Convention on International Trade in Endangered Species, came into effect in 1975, Mexico joined in 1991. So when the Mexican government said it would protect the turtle, Fredy and Maria are two of those who make sure it happens.

I watched Amor Real that evening over my verbena tea. I didn't follow the family feuds and romantic intrigue that well, there was too much past story, but it looked gorgeous, all bared chests and long curls, and that was the men. Long camera shots of dusty streets and heroes on gleaming stallions cut to close ups of women against antique interiors gazing from windows. Telenovelas were my new tutors testing my grammar and vocabulary. It was not difficult to understand the language as all the characters spoke in the imperative, 'Look at him!' or 'Say you love me', or 'Hold me.'

How I'd love to show off to my language tutor. He would be proud of me. 'Jorge! Recuerdame? Mira. Remember me? Look. I understand everything.'

The love affairs on hold until the following evening, it was time to get ready to go and meet Fredy and Maria. Even deprived of people, the cafe was civilization and disappeared when I walked through the coconut palms and sand plants and looked down the smooth creamy slope to the white breakers and deep Pacific blue. But this was the first time I walked beyond my cabin at night. I liked to sit outside it and smoke a cigarette before bed, and look at the black sky shimmering with diamond bright stars, the souls of ancestors in Mayan legend.

In my bamboo home I pulled on jeans, a shirt with sleeves, and set off into a transformed landscape. A mist hung low and obscured the beach that I thought I knew. Reminding myself to be practical, I looked for the thin white streak of sea on one side, an occasional glow of light on the other. I reckoned to walk straight ahead for about twenty minutes, but after a while it was hard to tell the beach from the sea or the night sky. There were no stars, no moonlight. I walked further into the smudgy dark, the sea lay quiet, there were no more waves, and I only knew my direction from the slope under my feet. My sense of time disappeared too. How would I tell when I reached the turtle centre? Would I see a light if I walked down by the sea edge?

I told myself to go back and ask Francisco to walk with me tomorrow night. Giving up didn't make it easier. Turning to go back, the way I had walked looked as strange as the way I had given up, the beach, the trees, the sea, had become a night world hostile and deceiving to casual intruders. I became anxious, unsure if I was even moving towards Marta's haven, anxious that I wouldn't recognise my cabin, my trees, the pattern where the vegetation became the one I saw every day. The wind got up and I was getting cold. It must be midnight by now. What if I went too far and alerted the bored soldiers at the lagoon point, was shot at for a turtle nest plunderer, a lost drug runner.

By day everything was clear again, the idea of losing myself foolish, but I checked out the research station to be completely sure, and it was visible from the beach. If a light shone there at night I must see it. Fredy and Maria had waited for me but were fine, 'see you tonight, then.'

So I set off again and I didn't ask Marta's husband. It seemed ridiculously simple in daylight, go straight along the beach until you get there. Did I walk further the next night? It felt like that but I still gave up like the heroine in a fable where the mist comes in every night to test her resolve. Francisco was awake, laughed at the idea of getting lost on the beach, and we returned, my third attempt, his bulging stomach led the way, hanging over light coloured shorts, the only thing I could see until the lights of the turtle station.

Fredy and Maria ran on Mexican time, slow and sure, something I still needed to remember. They were keen to talk before we set out, and as Maria handed me a coffee she asked where I'm from and what I was doing in Mexico, so far from my island. The next questions were not so predictable.

'Do you have terrorists in your country?'

The war was in Iraq, had not at that time transferred its horror into Britain. Terrorists, and I thought about the lengthy IRA struggle that had come to a delicate if official halt and the time I took students to the theatre in Piccadilly and there was a bomb warning for the West End of London. I thought about the thud and rattled kitchen window in my flat in Archway when I knew it was the blast of an explosion without ever having heard one before.

So I said, 'We had guerillas in one region for years.' This would make sense here in the state of Chiapas, home to the Zapatistas. 'In the end the government talked to them. It's ended now after thirty years. We have peace there. More or less.'

Fredy said, 'Some people here think the guerillas are a good thing.'

Maria moved on, 'How old do girls get married in your country?'

'They work and get married later, maybe thirty or older. My daughters had children in their thirties. I had them before I was twenty. It's changed a lot.'

'Here, girls get married when they are fifteen. Not all, but often they are very young. It isn't good.'

I didn't ask her how old she was when she married Fredy. Now I wish I had. But she must have studied before she married. My mind was one step behind.

Fredy threw me a quilted jacket, I noticed they wore seriously weather proof outfits. I put the jacket on and the hood up. Outside a red Honda beach buggy was ready. Maria and I sat on the back wheel racks, one either side, Fredy turned the ignition. We hummed along steadily looking for turtles, for the marks of egg sites. It was no longer a lagoon sandbar but the coast proper where mangroves edged the shore, a tangle of vegetation momentarily lit by the buggy lights.

After only ten minutes Fredy shouted pointing and we jumped off by a round patch of scraped sand as if children had been playing there. A wide wavy pattern stretched down to the water, an undulating profile of something more accustomed to the swell of sea. The biologists dropped to their knees digging their hands in, I joined in and about two feet down we uncovered a chamber of eggs, a mass of them, maybe seventy or eighty. They were hot and heavy, like shelled soft boiled eggs but round. We lifted handfuls into a woven plastic sack and the bag was put into an insulated box on the back of the buggy.

'Have to be kept warm,' Maria said over the wind and the engine noise.

We whizzed along, hunting for the next turtle nests, hardly nests, more like natural incubation pits. The wind hurled moths and specks of leaves and sand towards us. Dazzled crabs looked up from their holes. The headlights illuminated a nothingness of mist. My legs grew cold. I turned my head, it looked the same everywhere but Fredy drove steadily forward along the miles of beach.

Once or twice we stopped and looked at disturbed ground but found no more nests. We passed a few upturned fishing boats. Eventually the Honda turned and went back along the sea, our lights rippling over the water in the hope of seeing turtles coming ashore. Nothing. Then we moved back above the highest waterline. Fredy made an abrupt stop and turned to grab my arm, 'You see her?'

And there was a turtle still sloping down into the sand as she completed her clutch, too engrossed in this important work to look at us. Maria immediately started to excavate the eggs, digging inelegantly under her rear. The turtle began the next stage of her labours, flapping and patting the front of the nest, putting her potential offspring to bed tucking them up with her flippers, smoothing the sandy cover. Her face was solemn, reptilian.

'This one is young,' said Maria as she dug, 'they get much bigger.'

'Touch her, touch her,' encouraged Fredy, 'Don't be afraid, she won't hurt you.'

I put a hand on her shell and felt her bulk moving purposefully. Then I got down too and helped to undo all her effort. Fredy pushed her out of the way and she continued to smooth the sand nearby as we lifted out the precious store. I brought a new sack and the eggs, opaque and sandy, were rapidly transferred .

I felt blessed. I had witnessed one of the earliest creatures to have evolved, as she arrived from the water where all life began to repeat a cycle that encompassed the sea and the land. I had held the eggs fresh from her body, felt the heat that would transform them. Known as the 'grandmother of life' in Mexico, her eggs are considered aphrodisiac delicacies. Sympathetic magic food.

Seven years ago on a beach further north, a beach known for the large numbers of turtle nests, the same gangs that deal in illegal drugs carted away thousands of eggs on a night the beach was left unguarded. As Fredy said, 'people can be very bad.'

Eggs stored, we got back on the buggy and saw nothing more on the long ride back, and then I was outside my cabin and watched my companions turn back into the darkness. It was three a.m. as I took off my clothes and lay down on the canvas of my camp bed, my legs and back were stiff, stuck in sitting on the buggy position.

At breakfast Marta put scrambled eggs, frijoles, tortillas and cinnamon tea on the oilcloth covered table and asked about my night outing. 'And did they keep any to eat?' she asked. I laughed and said not as far as I knew.

It was the most alert I had seen her. She was always friendly, concerned I was comfortable and well fed but, like me, she suffered a surfeit of rest after a busy summer season. In between the minimum of activity since I was her only guest, Marta slumped in a hammock, a plump chrysalis. Now she began to emerge. She wiped fine sand from the cloth so my grand breakfast was set against a gleaming flowered surface and told me her son was coming to visit the next day, Saturday, the day I planned to leave. She also said that Francisco would take me into the mangroves by boat, later, when he returned from fishing.

The lancha made for the inland end of the lagoon and we passed the small group of houses, the fishing boats drawn up on the muddy bank opposite and slid along into a waterway bordered with roots. Mangrove roots rose up from brown water in twisting grey tangles. Francisco stood in the bow and I sat at water level and the roots rose above us and above them rose the trunks and foliage. I wanted it to be silent but the noise of the motor was loud.

After so much open space and the intense colour of beach and sea, this brown and dull green enclosed us, restful and secretive. Water and plants merged in dappled darkness. A black and white stork skimmed the surface and lifted to sit on the top of a tall tree, I looked through my binoculars but it was impossible to distinguish the exact branch, I didn't mind, I knew it was there. Three cormorants stood on a log. The pair of kingfishers, coloured grey and green like the man- groves, were unconcerned by the boat, there must be plenty of fish for everyone. All the birds in Boca del Cielo were fishing birds. These ones here where the river ran into the mangroves and the pelicans and frigate birds I watched dancing the waves every morning. Vultures were the one exception and even they ate fish, dead remains cast up on the sand or scraps from the fishermen's catch.

The fish themselves were more elusive. I only saw the shoals of tiddlers in the shallow waters of the lagoon, and the fish on my plate for lunch and dinner were flattened and fried or tucked inside a batter. I didn't know what the local fish looked like. They all tasted pretty much the same and as for Cecilia who recommended Marta's restau- rant I dispute her assertion that the food was good. The aroma and taste of prawn broth lingered from my first night. That was better than good, that was excellence. I wondered if turtles ate prawns.

Another military camp appeared, just a few olive green tents, and some army boats the same shape as the fishing lanchas, one whipped past us, small, dark and fast, soldiers staring. I was on a seaside holiday with soldiers among the mangroves and the coconut palms.

On the way back we stopped at the lagoon entry to the turtle station with its official sign, maybe this was Francisco's chance to check any signs of egg eating or egg availability. Fredy and Maria chatted to him and we all walked into the room on the ocean side to see the day's hatchlings. When he left, I stayed to catch up with every detail since they dropped me early that morning. I saw where the new nests were buried and dated in the net enclosure. It would be their time to run into the Pacific when I was back in Suffolk among the fire colours of an English Autumn.

Fredy and Maria were leaving that night for Tonala, picking up their daughter on the way. A *muchacho*, a youth, will be looking after the turtle centre. When I heard that, I thought how I turned back that night, how I could have missed my chance to take part for a moment in the kind of beach life that had gone on for thousands of years.

Maria took the bucket with the hatchlings; the sun dropped rapidly and it was time to let them respond to the call of the sea. We walked down to the sealine where frothy breakers rolling in from the rough deep became lacy frills around our bare feet. She tipped the clutch out slowly and they scrambled onto the wet sand. Frigate birds kept a distance. It was a good moment as storm clouds appeared and the wind was getting up. The birds flew out towards the horizon, the hatchlings rushed into the water and the sea lifted them away.

Fredy said these almost one day old turtles will return here to this beach when they are fifteen years old, to lay eggs in their turn. Biologists believe that a metallic mineral in the turtle's brain responds to the earth's magnetic field and that direction is set the moment the infant turtle struggles up through the sand. That is, they return if they survive to adulthood. And that possibility increases from 10% to 70% as a result of biologists and volunteers spending summer nights looking out for the armoured but land clumsy mothers, her eggs and bird snack offspring. What I wanted to know before Fredy and Maria left was what turtles ate.

'Do turtles eat prawns?'

'They do, crustaceans, molluscs, and most of all jellyfish.' Fredy said.

We hugged goodbye with a warm kiss on the cheek and hurried away, me along the beach, them to the mainland and the highway. Next day would take me back to the forested mountains and San Cristobal. There was nothing much to pack; leaves, shells, the patterned bone-like fragment whose identity I forgot to ask about, were my souvenirs.

The storm broke at 7.30 and I knew it was bad because Francisco turned the television off and then the lights went. But not so bad because I knew we would leave. Marta put a candle in a jar for me. I carried it to my cabin where I lay and watched and listened. Thunder and lightning coincided and I saw the palm trees bow down. I could not resist a look at the breakers and pushed against the wind to stand on the bank where the vultures spent their mornings. The sea was fearsome and the noise terrific.

Two hours later the storm moved out over the Pacific and the TV was on again. I smoked a cigarette, a cheap Ala sold singly, greedy to feel the intake of breath, the raw taste of nicotine, because I remembered the hurricane devastation ten years before on another beach in Mexico.

CHAPTER 17

The Heart is a Warrior

My leaving gift from Na Bolom was a print of a Trudy Blom photograph from the archive. It showed a cheerful Lacandon man exhaling from a large hand rolled cigar, forest grown tobacco. He leant back against a vine tangled tree in his white tunic, confident and at home. His face reminded me of the handsome blind man from Lacanha. The man in the print could be his father, the forest people were still few so they were certainly related. He seemed to be saying that even if it was time for me to leave, that the forest and he or someone like him, will still be there.

We sat at the long dining table, Fabiola, the garden staff and the house staff. They had half an hour off for the occasion. Summoned from library and laundry, workshop and office, Cecilia dressed for the cold as usual – I would miss our lunch time conversations in the library's shaded interior – Felicia in her blue nylon coat, quiet Javier in his favourite orange shirt, Na Bolom briefly closed down to say goodbye. We ate cake and drank fizzy drinks and I read the signed card full of messages saying they hoped we would meet again.

Fabiola's presence always created a rather formal atmosphere, no one forgot she was the directora with the power to hire and fire. I wished we were in the garden, chatting and joking. Manvel, urged to speak, looked abstracted and put upon. For the last time he sidestepped the position of head gardener. Again I took the initiative and said how much I valued the months of working alongside him, and the opportunities that Na Bolom had given me. Everyone smiled then looked serious as I took a photo of that final moment.

As my already former colleagues returned to their interrupted tasks, and I turned towards the open front door and a strangely empty afternoon, Ian called to me.

'I've put some of those things you wrote about the garden together with a few photographs,' and he put a folder into my hand. Before I could respond he disappeared back to his office. I sat down on a bench by the geraniums that grew so sturdy and red under Doña Bety's regime, and took out the two sheets of card. There were my words on the dye plants, the medicinal herbs and the orchids, a brief guide and record printed over a leaf rubbing background.

The passage of one volunteer was a momentary flutter in the life of Na Bolom so I was touched by Ian's gesture. He knew how much I wanted to leave something for visitors, that way of seeing I had learnt. But I smiled to see that what I took so seriously had part of a sentence missing and a photograph of an orchid just past its best. It really didn't need to be perfect, just like compost with pine needles. My work was at an end.

Officially I had left Na Bolom, but found myself gravitating there, unable to let go. My goodbye moment was over. Patricio called in the next day to see me and was told I'd left. When I heard this on one of my rather hang dog visits to the library, being there but not needed, I realised I must embrace the fact that my time at Na Bolom was complete, and decide how to mark this.

I found Patricio at home in the house with the palm tree. He was sympathetic to my lingering attachment but sensible, 'Na Bolom's garden, even Na Bolom and all it represents, isn't the whole of Chiapas, Bernardine. For you, it's the beating heart of your time here but remember those other times, the fiesta of San Lorenzo in Zinacantan, going to Oventik, and Boca del Cielo. And what about us, your friends?

Aren't you going to come back and see us? Na Bolom will carry on without you, but we will probably want to see you again. Now I'm finally going to take you out to eat the best meal in San Cristobal.'

I took Patricio's advice and thought about all the friends I'd made outside Na Bolom, Carolina, Tito, Jorge. I invited them for a last celebration on the night before I left San Cristobal. It was Carolina who gave me the best leaving gift I could have imagined. 'Bernardine, I have composta,' she said in her gravelly voice. 'I took off the box. Oh yes, that I don't forget about. The composta really worked. A few days ago I had the idea to clean the back patio. Before I did that, I thought I must try to turn the composta. I was always was afraid of doing it – so it became really big. It was so amazing. It really turned into earth. Of course I knew that it should work but I was afraid that when I turn it, everything will fall on the floor, but it was so concentrated that it stacked inside of the wood basket. it was wonderful earth.'

I gave Carolina such a hug. Moody, alarming Carolina who had softened so much since those early months I spent as her lodger. Typically, everyone met up at an inauguracion over wine and botanas, Carolina's favourite event. Tito had covered a wall with laser prints of roses, big, flamboyant, precision sharp.

We went off to eat quesadillas in Chilango's, in the Barrio Mexicanos, round the corner from my old room in Carolina's house, and then it was dancing at Club Latino. A night at Latino's was something I always meant to do and never got round to, but dancing with friends was the perfect way to spend the last night.

All of us jammed up close, we moved to merengue and cumbia from a nine piece band rich with brassy sounds and conga beats. And every time the band leader called out for the coletas or the conejos, the pigtails and the rabbits, I wanted to join in the competing roars from the San Cristobal locals and their rivals the weekending conejos up from Tuxtla, just for the joy of being here.

So I left Chiapas. Necklaces of amber and jade, fossil sap of trees and stone from the earth, and a soft string hammock, tucked into my luggage, the best presents for my family when I arrived home to another world. The bus journey took nineteen hours, and I needed that long, long drive away from the highlands through the many landscapes of Mexico.

At 1 a.m. under a black sparkly sky, the bus halted outside a roadside cafe, no houses or street lights just trees and darkness all around. Stepping out into the hot humidity of another state, the feel of the air on my skin told me we had descended into the lowlands. Long, high wheeled trucks droned along the highway and we had another eight hours to go.

As we crossed the state borders soldiers boarded and scrutinised proof of identity. At one border soldiers stood over two young men, my neighbours in the seats across the aisle. They brought out papers and offered them to the soldiers pointing to words which explained where they went to school and what their fathers' work was. The bus listened.

Although they were from Chiapas they could have been illegal migrants from Guatemala. Their features were Mayan, like the frescoes at Bonampak in Chiapas and the carvings at Tikal over the national border in Guatemala. Round faces with curved lips, like Romeo who played guitar at Adelina's restaurant and whose family fled Guatemala during the long terror of the 1980s and 90s. Eventually, the border guards were satisfied, the young men smiled and all the passengers relaxed. Then my tooth fell out. Not a real tooth but a cap. Even so it felt significant as if it waited until it was safe to fall apart, on my way home. A small event that eased me away from Chiapas and ushered me towards my everyday life.

First I passed through one of the largest cities on the planet; 25 million people live in Mexico's capital. Mexico City, or DF as it's popularly known, – DF for Distrito Federal – is set in a bowl, a wet basin rapidly drying and cracking under this vast population, and covered with a smog sent up by heat of their activity.

The modern city grew out of the Aztec city, Tenochtitlan, near the great flower gardens and orchards of Moctezuma and near the poet king Nezahualcoyotle's residence which directly inspired the botanical gardens of Europe. The Aztecs had a god of flowers, Xochipilli. Warriors fought 'flower battles' to capture sacrificial prisoners and Royal Aztec ambassadors presented bouquets to the Spanish.

'There is welcome here, in this flowering land where no one can destroy the flowers and the songs. They will endure in the house of the Giver of Life.' Ayuocuan, Aztec poet.

It was hard to believe his joyful words when the bus passed through so many traffic lanes and spreading settlements as we crept into the city. The only earth was in the unmade roads puddled from rain among haphazard houses. These were the poor outskirts constantly replenished by migrants from the country. Further into the city, DF's colonial districts still had courtyards flowery with jacaranda and fruitful with fig trees, and eventually the bus swept along wide highways into the centre where ahuehuetes dominated, cypress trees with enormous thick trunks and arched branches, living remnants from the time of the Aztecs.

Hernan Cortes sat under an ahuehuete and wept after a defeat and massacre, a Spanish defeat before the final destruction of the Aztec empire. Two volcanoes, Popocatepetl and Ixtacihuatl rose in the distance. The former is erect, male, active, occasionally erupting and the latter a reclining female shape, dormant. Typically, the love of these two godly beings, according to legend, is a doomed one, simmering and frustrated.

After the small human settlements of Chiapas the magnitude and extremes of the capital were new to me, the imprint of a violent history on an extraordinary setting displayed as our insect coach hurried inward.

My feet were numb from the long bus journey, longer than it would take to fly from Mexico to London. They livened up as I walked from bus station to metro. Elisa had invited me to stay with her before I caught the plane. She was living with her parents just outside Mexico City, in Toluca, a town not yet subsumed into the metropolis.

Toluca was restful and we spent a few days catching up; I was happy to see that the eternal revolutionary, Cesar, had been demoted to a friendship level and that Rodrigo replaced him in Elisa's heart. Rodrigo was her secret for the time being. In Toluca she maintained a careful balance of independence and family harmony.

When her mother and I sat at the table after breakfast and talked, she asked me about Elisa's admirers. 'But do these men respect her?'

I said that no man would dare attempt anything that Elisa did not tolerate, and added that no one could have anything but admiration for her daughter. In my way, I was as watchful over Elisa's passions as her mother.

I brought out small souvenirs from Chiapas, a round box made from leaves and flowers mashed and reformed into rigid paper, black with a red heart on the lid. It made me think of the book of Mayan heart metaphors, 'the heart is a warrior.' That was what I wanted her mother to see, but it's hard for mothers to understand that quality in their own child. The box was filled with shells from the beach at Boca del Cielo.

Elisa showed me her recent photographs. As I looked through the images, all taken in the maternity ward of a public hospital here in the city, Elisa selected those she wanted to enter for a competition, Women's Lives, put on by a human rights organisation. She chose one of a sixteen year old girl with her twin babies. The young mother sat on the edge of a hospital bed and looked out, unsmiling and still, as if she's seeing the life before her. Two swaddled packets lay on the bed beside her. We called the picture, 'Mother of Two at Sixteen,' and chose another entry.

Another baby also wrapped securely lay in his mother's lap. The woman gazed at him in that way new mothers do, drinking them in, wanting to know them and who they will be. All the mothers and babies wore the same white hospital cotton. They were not from comfortable families, or they would not be here in the free maternity ward. This young mother had long wavy hair like Botticelli's Venus and her face was covered with blotchy freckles like a map of islands.

We delivered the photographs to a building with a security check at the entrance. The man in front of us lay a hand gun on the counter which the guard tagged and put it in a cubby hole and did the same for our bags without any sign of this incongruity. The human rights offices on the fifth floor were untidy and the people friendly, the photographs were handed over and I felt a contact surge of happiness from Elisa's relief that she had made her choice and brought it into the world.

Along with Rodrigo, Elisa kept her other photography, her work for the EZLN magazine Rebeldia and their website, as part of her other life. She folded her arm in mine and made me promise not to mention this in front of her parents. Then she reverted to her lighthearted self.

'I still don't see him, you know, that man,' she joked, and I knew it wasn't the evasive Cesar she was talking about. 'Even when it's so hot and we are all sweating, he is still in that mask. You want to come with me and look at that?'

'Yes, Elisa, how can I not want to see that man, that you talked about so much. Even more than you talked about Cesar. Remember him?'

So we set off to Huixquilucan to see Marcos. We travelled by metro, bus and finally taxi up through pine woods to get to Huixquilucan, the place of the thistle, about an hour and a half from the capital.

Was this important, to see for myself, since the man himself insisted it was the ideas and experience of all those men and women at Oventik and elsewhere that were important. Those people behind their black balaclavas and red paisley neckerchiefs, that mattered, not this unknown masked man, reputed to be a doctor of philosophy.

'Somos todos Marcos' We are all Marcos, said one of the tee shirts on the market stall outside the Santo Domingo church in San Cristobal, where inside, men sought powerful help from another world by shaking pox over the saints in their velvet robes. 'Somos todos Marcos'. But there had to be a first Marcos, the one who had the courage to begin. Or was Marcos an idea, a concept. Perhaps there wasn't a single actual person who was Marcos.

These thoughts came to mind only when I stood looking up at a man dressed in army fatigues, balaclava and khaki cap. He looked like all the newspaper photos, the screen printed tee shirts, the man in the films I saw during San Cristobal's Human Rights week in April.

Elisa and I stood under a tarpaulin in a field along with hundreds of others as the rain poured down. We were a long way in place and time from Oventik, this was another rural parish but high above Mexico City. Huixquilucan was hosting a 'dialogue'.

Marcos and the small group of committed supporters that travelled with him, the 'zapatur', arrive in a small town or rural community, and locals talk about the important issues of their area which may be land evictions or being refused permission to sell flowers on the street. The people here were mainly Otomi Indian, and they had plenty to talk about, nervous of the city so hungry for land and water. Mexico City has sucked out the lake under its foundations and the oldest buildings have sunk so deep they lean like war damaged targets. Inexorably, the city turns to see what it can devour next.

At the stage edge a queue formed, each person, women as well as men, with something to say, losing the pieces of land that sustained them, replaced by planning permission for a private airport; water company concessions; and the small farmers of San Juan Yautepec in the vicinity of Huixquilucan moved out while development took place for the 'millionaires'.

A man jumped his turn leaping onto the stage to make a passionate rant in Otomi. And every so often a steward moved across to poke the tarpaulin and shoot a stream of water from above Marcos' head onto the grass. Two little girls sang a welcome song. All this time, Marcos said nothing. He listened like I've never seen anyone listen. Occasionally, he leant forward to make a note, or stood to shake hands, he accepted the poncho an elderly man took off to give him and was embraced by another. Then I knew there was one Marcos.

After everyone had spoken, he came to the front of the stage, removed his pipe and began. 'We are the guardians of the mountains and the forests and the rivers. We need to see all these problems we have heard about today as a whole. It is the system that must change. '

Of course. Now the name Marcos made sense.

It was our turn and we listened to him; locals, the supporters from the city, the taxi driver with his zapatista star swinging on the windscreen, Elisa with her camera recording it all. I wondered to Elisa why there were no police here,

'There are,' she replied, 'just not in uniform.'

The EZLN is not a political party and wasn't seeking election. There were no promises, no campaign speeches, no one to vote for. There were the 'dialogues', that rare listening, where Marcos' presence was a catalyst, creating an opportunity for local people to speak out, and drawing an audience so the speakers were heard. Marcos ended with, 'We must transform from within, we are for everyone, but we begin with the jodidos.'

We lingered on after Marcos was whisked away in a minibus, waiting for the crowds to clear, Elisa got us a lift with Juan, Carlos and Victor a photographer for the one newspaper that reported Zapatista events.

A steady rain fell on umbrellas and plastic bag hats. I sat sideways in the back seat squeezing water from the ends of my hair, glad I brought a jacket. Elisa took out a tiny mirror and curled her eyelashes with a teaspoon, her reassuring beauty pack, while Victor loaded pictures onto his laptop and selected which ones to send off for tomorrow's issue.

I wanted to check what exactly this word, *jodido*, meant. The 'why-were-we-born people,' said Elisa.

'those who have nothing, no resources to help themselves,' offered Juan. Carlos steering between people and cars turned to add his interpretation.

'It comes from 'to be a nuisance'. The jodidos are the nuisance, those who disturb us.'

September in the capital was mild and on my last day Elisa wanted to introduce me to her landscape, and I began to see a gracious city even though it was crammed with people and traffic. I also began to understand the contradictory nature of DF residents; Elisa, Adriana and Miguel, all working at Na Bolom, all from the capital, chilangos, fast talkers, impatient and passionate. How unlike the Chiapanecos, laid back, amiable, going their own way with quiet determination.

We walked across the great expanse of square in front of the imposing buildings of cathedral and parliament. This square that I have seen in so many photographs and film clips. We were upright specks on the empty background, tiny and exposed. An enormous Mexican flag rose above us. Only a great mass of people could dare to stand here and challenge the twin powers of god and government. And they have done so and still did.

In front of parliament a marquee housed a group of Triqui Indian families on a permanent human rights demonstration. David and Goliath. I passed by and saw a whole village life enacted under canvas, tables and cooking, with blankets neatly piled up for the night. Women went in and out with babies and bags of food.

God too was challenged by human actions; the cathedral was propped up with wooden buttresses and a notice explained how subsidence had caused dangerous changes to parts of the structure.

Eventually, I had my fill of the historical culture Elisa thought I should know about; the art exhibition devoted to volcano paintings in the Palace of Fine Arts, and the heroic murals by Orozco in Sanborns restaurant. We moved away from the city centre and wandered along checking the street sellers. The pavements were lined with stalls; juiced fruit drinks, a bookseller practicing his guitar, a flag seller with streams of green, white and red plastic, it was almost Independence Day.

Elisa clicked her camera on the tacos stand, as crisp vegetables with a dollop of yogourt were rolled into fresh pancakes. We entered the covered market and sat up at a counter, ordered fruit drinks green from cactus pads or like sunsets from mangoes and oranges, and ate from the comida del dia. It was cool under the matting roof and we exchanged incitements to remember this or that.

Elisa wanted to show me a photography exhibition nearby and see her former professor in the university department attached to the gallery. Many of the photographs were dramatic, shocking; gross couplings by spectacularly obese bodies in a brothel, forensic pictures of shootings and real police chases. Elisa disapproved of these in your face statements, 'Just a sort of porno, those photographers think the people looking at their pictures are stupid too.'

I looked and looked at one. A young man lay on a mortuary trolley, his body huge like a giant, the skin taut. Notes next to the picture said that he drowned, believed to have been hit over the head and thrown into the sea at Mazunte, a few miles north of Boca del Cielo.

Mazunte was the main nesting beach for golfina turtles, an *arribada* beach, and one that used to be the site of a regular harvest of turtle meat and egg collecting complete with on site processing factory. Under the CITES agreement it became a protected area. Volunteers patrolled the beach during the summer nesting season and a military presence in the area deterred blackmarket activity.

Elisa explained that the verdict of accidental death by drowning had been challenged by the family who arranged the autopsy I saw before me. I knew from watching television news in Mexico that there was often a divergence of opinion between official and common knowledge.

The image stayed with me, this smooth, brown, blown up body of a man washed in from the sea, photographed from above, chest open displaying his heart.

I sat and read a copy of a newspaper article which reported that this man and his girl friend, both students at the university in Mexico City, stayed on at the beach for a few days after other volunteers left. Gangs of egg thieves arrived with lorries. An estimated million eggs were dug out of the sand that night and, unofficially, it's believed the lovers were witnesses in the way of a lucrative opportunity. The girl's body has never been found.

After the volcano exhibition, the gun checked in at the office door and the autopsy photo, I was whisked off to meet Rodrigo in his flat in Coyoacan. Of all the places I had seen in this grand and extraordinary city, the garden squares of Coyoacan were calm and reassuring. Unlike the dominating scale of the central square these were a balance of buildings and nature, short avenues and pockets of enticing seclusion. Here were trees and flowers, balloon sellers and coffee stalls, elderly people practising ballroom steps in the 'place of the coyotes'.

Rodrigo was lively and cheerful, a grown up man with a job as well as a photograph of Che on the wall. His thick black hair was tied back and his arms constantly reached for Elisa.

'Have you eaten mole, Bernardine? It's not a dish you find in Chiapas, more popular in lowland Mexican. We will eat chicken mole tonight.'

The first time I ate chicken mole, pronounced molay, I looked in disgust at the fat leg draped with a thick brown sauce. I quickly learnt how delicious it was. Mole is made from chile and chocolate, rich and reputedly aphrodisiac, and while Rodrigo and Elisa busied themselves in the open plan kitchen I put on a CD I bought on the metro. I liked this way that shopping came to me. The unemployed migrants invented a thousand tiny enterprises to survive. They moved from carriage to carriage, often identifiably rural in checked shirts and cowboy hats. Bags and trays held their pirated CDs and DVDs, packets of sweets, nuts or healing herbs.

This particular CD was a patriotic compilation timely put together for the Independence Day celebrations. The cover was red, white and green, the national colours with the national symbols; an eagle, a snake, oak leaves and cactus against a web of lines like crackling on a dry land. At the first track, Viva Mexico, I felt tearful. I was leaving a place and people who gave me a renewed sense of life. I wanted to go home and I wanted to take that with me. One of the great things about 'away' is how it imbues 'home' with a fresh vision. All the inward clutter had fallen away, at least temporarily, and the well of energy was full and sparkling with immediacy.

The concept of humans as one species among many, brings with it the idea that a life of separation from these other species, plants and animals, is a deprivation and we suffer a loss. A loss that may be so gradual and bound up with the growth of urban living and indoor work that it is attributed to other causes, housing, education, divorce. The residue of a connection to the natural world is in our human need for pets, now called companion animals, or an office atrium filled with trees and plants.

It wasn't just the being 'away' that had affected me, it was the immersion in the forests of another landscape that I carried home to my own Suffolk woods. For some people and at certain times this immersion becomes a craving like pregnancy cravings, urgent and apparently irrational. When I read that there was an academic word for this necessity for the wilderness, for closeness to other species, it made sense. Biophilia is an ugly word for something that brings a sense of harmony. An ugliness redeemed because I find it in my favourite companion book where Les Beletsky explains;

> 'The concept of biophilia says that, for our own mental health we need to preserve some wildness in the world. Because people evolved amid rich and constant interaction with other species and natural habitats we have deeply ingrained tendencies to affiliate with other species and an actual physical need to experience, at some level, natural habitats. This instinctive, emotional attachment to wildness means that if we eliminate species and habitats, we harm ourselves because we will lose things essential to our mental well being.'

These things filled my mind while I sat with Rodrigo and Elisa in one of the Coyoacan squares at dusk after our meal. We watched the dancers set up their places, greet each other, change to loose trousers and tie on ankle rattles. The three big drums started to resonate calling attention, the charcoal burner was lit and lumps of copal resin thrown on. People gathered and a cloud of sweet scented smoke drifted among us. The inner circle stood ready and an older Indian man led an invocation turning to north, south, west and east. We, the outer circle, the onlookers, men, women, lots of children, dogs, felt the sounds reverberate inside our chests, the thump of heart beat expand. A little boy moved by the drums, turned and leapt as the dancers did.

I remembered my mother's stories of dancing as a girl at the Saturday night crossroad ceilis in Ireland. I remembered sitting by the River Lea, alongside bottles and shopping trolleys, as it flowed through East London while my son flicked a rod and line over the thick water. Not far from the River Lea, my aunties' allotment, remains a part of me, an allotment enriched with my shovel of manure from the bread-van horse that did the rounds of post war housing.

The more we are separated from what was part of our grandparents' and ancestors' daily life, the potato planting at Easter, chickens in the yard, gathering mushrooms and wood, the local names of trees and birds, then the more we lack an understanding of our place in the universe. This is why I'm a gardener rather than a garden designer. I need the used muscles, the mud on my hands, touching, observing, breathing the scents, feeling with everything I've got even to the scratches and stings. I need to know I am not mistress of any universe but a willing and active participant.

That's why my eldest grandson said to his younger sister to remind her how much she would like staying with me, 'We can do jobs, Anna!'

And they do, just like their mother did. Not cosmetic ones or because it's 'educational' but ones with a cause and effect, they carry in the wood and sit by the fire, compete to grab the potatoes as the fork unearths them, and eat them for supper. I know that this changes and they won't stay enamoured of 'jobs' but it will stay in them somewhere. Their actions are laid down in them like a layer of sediment in the earth tells the history of that exact moment, part of the composition of that landscape outer or inner, and is ready to be tapped sometime in the future.

In Coyoacan I watched the dancers whirl faster, circling as we do in the universe, leaping for the sky and crouching to the earth. The drums told them how to move, held them steady. Some of the men took off their shirts and sweat gleamed on chests, some retired and others took their place, a stocky grandmother moved in her long skirts without apparent effort. There were those who danced the steps and those who let go and then the dance danced them. The grandmother, I knew, was one of those who had the dances in her from childhood.

A big woman turning with ease as the drum rhythms called up the movements.

The spectrum of Mexican people was here in the dancers and the watchers. Here were the Indian, the mixed descendants of Spanish and Indian, and other later immigrants subsumed into being Mexican, but often identifiably ex Irish, Russian, Lebanese.

'Time to go, Bernardina,' Elisa said, taking charge of my ridiculously small suitcase on wheels, and I hugged Rodrigo and thanked him for such a delicious hospitality, the sweet and the hot, a perfect last taste of Mexico. And then we walked away to the metro and the airport.

Checked in, I turned to take in a glimpse of Elisa hanging over the barrier, waving, before I walked through into the departures lounge. I held the round basket from Lacanha and inside it was Elisa's present to me, a painted clay 'tree of life', speciality of Toluca.
In my notebook she had written,

'Don't worry, Bernardina, you won't forget. We carry the forests in our hearts.'

chok
scattering

To order copies of Garden of the Jaguar

WEBSITE: www.bernardinecoverley.co.uk

EMAIL: bernardine5@btinternet.com

N.B. spelling of bernardine

REFERENCE

A Flower Lover's Guide to Mexico by Phil Clark
pub Minutiae Mexicana.

Tribes and Temples by Frans Blom
pub The Tulane University of Louisiana, New Orleans.

People of the Bat – Dreams & Tales from Zinacantan by Robert M.
Laughlin 1988
pub. Smithsonian Institute

The Flowering of Man – A Tzotzil Botany of Zinacantan vol 1& 2 by
Dennis Breedlove & Robert M. Laughlin, abridged edition
pub. Smithsonian Institute

Linda Schele drawing collection and John Montgomery glyphs
at www.famsi.org

The Last Lords of Palenque by Victor Perera and Robert D. Bruce
University of California Press

Zapata by John Steinbeck pub Penguin Classics

The Rough Guide to the Mayan World 2nd edition

The Ecotravellers Wildlife Guide to Tropical Mexico by Les Beletsky
pub Academic Press, Harcourt, Brace & Co

Plantas Curativas de Mexico by Dr Luis G.Cabrera

The Maya Guide by Daniela Rodriguez Herrera & Enrique Franco
Torrijos
pub Minutiae Mexicana

www.worldlandtrust.org

CREDITS

The jaguar on the book cover is adapted from a drawing by Frans Blom of a carving on the Mayan site of Chichen Itza. Permission to use gratefully received from Na Bolom.

Permission gratefully received from Les Beletsky to quote the biophilia paragraph in his Ecotravellers Wildlife Guide to Tropical Mexico, and from John Myers to use his drawing of the ceiba tree.

Permission from Kevin P Groark to quote from his paper, Willful Souls: Dreaming and the Dialectics of Self-Experience among Tzotzil Maya of Highland Chiapas, Mexico

The glyphs, hul, arrival and chok, scattering, and the jaguar drawing are from the extraordinary collection at FAMSI © Foundation for the Advancement of Mesoamerican Studies, Inc. www.famsi.org. Thank you.

All photographs by author. Author photograph Lynne Ward.